Maggie was raised in Glasgow; she had a very ordinary secondary school education. She married and supported her husband in his career until the loss of her children changed her life and she found herself working as a book-keeper for various companies in England.

Maggie Colombe

HOW HE ROBBED ME OF MY THREE BABY DAUGHTERS

AUSTIN MACAULEY PUBLISHERS™

LONDON • CAMBRIDGE • NEW YORK • SHARJAH

A CIP catalogue record for this title is available from the British Library.

ISBN 9781786938879 (Paperback)
ISBN 9781786938886 (E-Book)
www.austinmacauley.com

First Published (2017)
Austin Macauley Publishers Ltd.
25 Canada Square
Canary Wharf
London
E14 5LQ

Dedication

To my three daughters: Ann, Grace and Joy.

Acknowledgements

My grateful thanks to the very many kind people who helped me through this very difficult time of my life!

Table of Contents

Introduction

We met again **seventeen** years after the day that you were taken from the home that we lived in. When my children were taken from me, Ann, who was my oldest daughter, was five years old, my middle daughter Grace was about three and a half and my baby Joy was around one-year-old at the time that this happened to us.

I do love you all very much, you have all grown up, and you have had your lives to live. Ann and Joy, you both have two lovely children, whom I know you love very much. Grace seems to have been very successful in her career, and as far as I can see, you are all happy and successful individuals.

Your father, who decided (with the help of course from other people) to take you away from me, seemed to think that I could or should be able to live without you. He obviously was not prepared to do this himself, and leave me to bring you up; in spite of the fact that he was besotted with the girl of fourteen and a half that he had run away with a few months before. He had both me and many other people fooled over his relationship with the girl for a very long time.

Some people who have been in the news in recent years have unwittingly taken advantage of youth, albeit the youth in question were hanging about looking like adults, and because they looked and behaved the part, their ages were not in question at the time that this happened.

There are also some other people though, who do irreparable damage by the way they creep along insidiously, they use their charm on unsuspecting parents and on vulnerable children, the end result is the same of course, but the difference is that one action was deliberately and cunningly planned, while the other was not!

Over the years, many people who met me and knew that my children were taken abroad by their father would ask me if he was foreign, but no, he was born in Hessle in Hull, his parents were both English and they moved to Scotland to live when he was about three years of age.

Why then did he flee the country and come back later and take my children abroad? Was it because I was a bad wife and mother? Was it because I did not love or want my children with me? The answer was of course that he had to flee from the consequences of the life that he was living.

How did I cope? The only way was to stop myself from having any emotional feelings towards you all, as thoughts about you always brought me to tears no matter where I was at the time. This was the hardest thing that I have had to do in my entire life!

There is no greater loss than the loss of a child, except of course when you lose all of them!

My story then is about some of the bends that I went through, and how and why I lost all of my family.

Visiting my grandparents in Cardros

Chapter 1
My Life in Scotland

I thought that I would start this story from the beginning, and that I would cover some of my childhood, your father's childhood in as much as I know it, how we both met, and when things started to go wrong in our relationship.

I was born in Glasgow where I lived with my mother and my two sisters. One of my sisters was older than me, and at that time I had one sister who was younger than me.

I have realised over the years that my mother (for her own reasons) had locked out of her mind so many of the things that had happened to her; she sadly went to her grave full of all of her secrets, and with all of the questions that I had about myself, and us as a family unanswered.

This is the reason that I have taken the time to write this book, because I don't know how many years that I have left of my own life, and I want my children to know all of the facts about their life, and as far as I know, where they came from.

When I met my children again after seventeen years, they did ask me the questions about what had happened to our family, but I felt at the time that I could not explain in a few words some of the many things that had taken years to happen to us. This is why I have taken the time now to put into writing these things that they wanted to know, as their lives will continue after I am gone.

My mother was a very ordinary but a very hard working person. She was brought up in the country, and I understood from some of my relatives that my mum was an attractive young woman, because I was told by a member of the family that my mum had been the belle of the village that she had grown up in. Sadly, because of the things that were happening in her own life, when she was a young woman of about seventeen years old, and because of the generation thing that was prevalent at this time, and might I add 'the pride' in families at that time, she was told to leave her home.

It was then that she had no alternative but to go to live in what was the nearest big city to where she had been brought up, and that city was Glasgow in Scotland. I understand that my grandfather was very strict towards his children at that time.

As I grew up, I believed that my mum was a very strong person. Perhaps this is not surprising; she was a young country girl, and she suddenly had to face a completely different life in the big smoke of the City of Glasgow, with what would seem to be a family on the way. I know that my mum had her first daughter when she was around eighteen years of age.

You know my mum didn't say very much to me as I was growing up, about what happened to her in her life. But I can clearly remember something that she did say to me, and this was many years before I lost my family - she believed that the sins of the fathers are visited upon the next and even sometimes the next generation. Now my mum was not a Christian, she never did express any religious views to me, but I remember that she said this to me on one occasion when we were together.

Very interesting, when you think of what happened in my life, and to my family!

It is so very strange that I spent my childhood with her, and yet, I find it hard to describe my relationship with her. To me, she was always in charge of what went on within the immediate family. She was a very attractive looking person. I remember a close male friend of mine who came to a family wedding many years later, saying to me that my mum was a much more attractive looking person than I was. She was also full of work ethic, and she most certainly did the maximum she could for us as a family.

I thought the world of my mum, even although, as we all do, she made her mistakes, she will always be so very special to me, and I would take my hat off to her at any time!

Now I can remember the first time that I met any of my relatives. As I said, my mum was sent away from her home as a young woman. I am sure though that she missed her family very much, as she had three sisters, and she had been very close to them as she grew up. And she must also have missed the lovely area that she had been brought up in. And that was probably the reason that she took us there that day, on a trip to the sea shore in the village of Cardross where she had been brought up.

So there we were sitting on the lovely beach enjoying the sunshine, when just by accident some of our relatives walked past us, and they saw us sitting there on the beach. And this was the start of many trips that we took there, to see and get to know my mother's family.

I think that perhaps that this was the time that I had an accident on the beach, I was running along and landed on a piece of broken bottle that someone had left, and I had a nasty cut on my foot (I still have the scar) and I had to go to the local hospital. Anyway everyone rushed around, and I was given the necessary medication and stitches. I know that after this accident I was in a wheelchair until I could walk on my foot again.

I think that it was at this time that I met my really nice grandparents. That was the first time I remember meeting any of our relatives, and from this time on, one of the things that was always a highlight in my childhood were the times that we would spend with our relatives in Cardross. My mother was the eldest in an all-girl family. When we met up with them, two of her sisters were married and had their own families, and the one who had a paralysed arm from birth always lived at home with her parents.

Now apart from our family living in the city, my relatives all lived within a four-mile radius of each other, and that was why it made it even more special for us when we went down there to visit with them. We had some lovely times there when we met up with our aunts and uncles and their families. I can still remember inheriting a red train that was discarded by my cousin, and I was able to take this home with me. And we were also given some other toys that we were able to take home with us. This was very special to us as we didn't have many toys at that time.

This is the place that stands out the most in my childhood memory; it is the village of Cardross. It was (and I think still is) a small village in Dumbartonshire in Scotland. It has a rail link to Glasgow, and it has the most lovely of beaches. I know that my older sister loved this place as much as I did, we so loved it there with our relatives!

The village of Cardross is also only about four miles from the seaside town of Helensburgh, and it is on the West Coast of Scotland. I think that it was there in Helensburgh that my mum would have met my father. Apparently my mother worked in service for one of the big houses in Helensburgh, and my father was brought up there.

It is amazing the silly little memories that we all have, I can remember sitting in a café in Glasgow with my mum and my sisters, we were all sitting there waiting to go on the train to Cardross. At the time we decided that we would have some refreshments before our train journey. I can still remember being teased many times in my young life, because when we had a cake to eat with a cherry stone in it, rather than take the cherry stone out of my mouth and put this on the side of my plate as most people would do, I decided to swallow it. I think that this sums me up as a person, always apologetic and unsure of myself!

All of these visits, when we went to meet with members of our family, became so very special to me and my sisters. I have so many fond memories of the times that we would leave Glasgow and go to visit with my relatives. I remember sitting in my grandfather's lovely garden, and we were enjoying eating the raw vegetables that he had grown. It seemed to me that the sun always shone when we went there. My granddad's garden was always as pretty as a picture, as he always kept it immaculate (unlike me with mine today). Usually on the way home my grandma would give us a big bag of sweets to eat. What a treat!

My grandparents will always be special to me, they were such nice people, and I will always think of them with much affection and love!

So my mother's parents, your great-grandparents, lived in the village of Cardross in Dumbartonshire. They lived a short walk from the beach, and we would go to the beach to play each time that we visited them. Sometimes we would walk miles along the beach to collect the bottles that people had left after they had their picnics. The owner of the shop where we took them back to at the time would always give us a few pennies for returning the empty bottles to the shop.

When we were children, my lovely mother could not afford to take us away on any holidays, as we were always very poor in our family. I think that this was the reason that made it more of a treat for us when we went to see our relatives. I know that Cardross will always have a big place in the hearts of my sisters, as well as me.

My granddad was amazing, or so I thought anyway; although I didn't get the opportunity to hear him play it (which I now regret), I was told that he could play the piano that they still had in the living room of their home. He also grew the most beautiful prize flowers, and each year my uncle who lived in Helensburgh would take his flowers to various flower shows, and I was told that my uncle won many prizes for my grandad's prize dahlias at these exhibitions. When my grandfather went out to work, he was employed by British Rail, and his job was to man the signal box at Cardross railway station, both during this time, and also in the war time.

He loved his modest home, and his wife and family. As well as the lovely flowers that he grew, he also grew many different kinds of vegetables in his large garden. When he was crippled in later life with arthritis; he still had a weed free garden by crawling along the ground to do the weeding!

My grandmother was only a housewife (I say only) but you know what I mean. When we went to stay with them my grandma would always go to the nearby farm and collect new eggs, she would also buy fresh rolls from the baker, and she would fill the rolls with scrambled eggs for us to eat. I have never tasted such a nice breakfast as that was. I remember also that when she cooked our dinner for us, she always cooked the fresh peas and other vegetables that my grandfather grew in the garden that he loved.

My granddad sometimes called me Greta, he could not always remember the pet name of Rita that I had been given. So I now get called Margaret, Maggie, Magz and even Rita. I have learned to respond to all of these names over the years. My granddad also had a nickname for me, he called me Stage Struck Fanny, because I always wanted to go on the stage and sing.

As you can tell from my granddad's name for me, as I was growing up, the main thing that I enjoyed doing was singing. I really did want to go on the stage and entertain people. My grandfather was right about me; I did have the bug. I really did want to go on the stage, and this was because I loved to sing and dance and entertain people.

I think that I would have got this idea in my head after my mum took me as a young child to various variety concerts in the theatres of Glasgow. I loved it when the men and women got on to the stage and started to sing and dance. I really did want to be up there doing this with them. As a result of this, I am afraid that this was the thing that I wanted to do the most with my life.

Unfortunately for me though, my mother did not discuss with me any of the details about my own father. The only knowledge that I have of him was from my older sister's birth certificate, or from the little bit of information from within our family; and also from the information that I found out when I visited the births, marriages and deaths register in the city of Edinburgh, which I did later on in my life. One thing I did know was that my two sisters and I had the same father. I will never know however why my father's name was not put on to my birth certificate.

But what do I know then about my father, your grandfather? I know that he was also a Scotsman, and he had been brought up in the seaside town of Helensburgh on the West Coast of Scotland. And Helensburgh is only about four miles from where my mum was brought up in Cardross. Apparently my dad was an electrician by trade, and he was also a lay preacher. I have no idea though what his religious beliefs could possibly have been, as he didn't help my mum in any way at all with our upbringing.

I grew up wanting to know who my father was, but by the time I was old enough to think seriously about this, and to think that I could perhaps meet up with him, he had already died. It was sadly too late for me to meet with him. I will always regret this!

I do not even have any recollection of meeting my father's parents. I would like to be able to tell you about your great-grandparents on my father's side, but the only information that I have was that my grandfather was a civil engineer. Although I do not know it, I would think that my grandmother was a housewife, as most wives did not go out to work in those days. I do know that being a civil engineer was a really good job to have in those days.

One of the things that I did get to find out was that my own father was ten years older than my mum, that he had a marriage and family prior to being with my mum, and he also had another family later when he and my mother separated. The only other thing that I know about him is his surname.

It is true that as a young child, I would have loved to have known my real father, I had two step-fathers, and I know that neither of them were suitable partners for my very hard working mother.

When I was growing up, I was not called by my father's surname, and most of my life I felt guilty because I understood that I was illegitimate. Someone said to me that at the time that I was born, the government started to help and support women who were on their own with children. It was suggested to me that this was perhaps the reason that my father's name was not on my birth certificate. But I will never know the truth about this; I no longer have a problem with this; people look at things so differently now; and in any case it would not have been me who ought to feel guilty about this.

Now I think that at some time in my very young childhood, I went to live with my aunt and uncle in Helensburgh, and just by coincidence this was also where my father came from. I am sure that I heard that I had stayed there with them for a time. This would also explain the reason that I got the nickname of Rita, because my aunt and uncle had a daughter of their own called Margaret, my birth name. I can vaguely remember being brought by them to the first address that I remember that we lived in. This was in a place called Govan, and this was within the City of Glasgow. I think that this was before we met them on the beach. So as you can tell there are quite a number of blanks in my brain about my young childhood.

The first street that I remember as a child then, was this house that I was brought to as a child in Vicarfield Street, in the Govan area of Glasgow. Perhaps I previously stayed in Helensburgh because my mum was having another baby, but I do not remember what happened at all.

But I can remember living in Vicarfield Street fairly well. We lived in a rented house that I would call a flat today, and my mum rented this from a 'factor' at that time. The flat was in the downstairs part of a large tenement building, it had one living room which I think if I remember correctly was also the kitchen, and this room also had a recess for a bed in there. It had one other separate bedroom, and the toilet facilities were on the outside part of the building. We must have lived there for quite a number of years, as I know that we left there when I was around about eleven years of age.

One of the things that still sticks out in my mind was that the children who were playing outside our house would often chalk on the outside walls of our home, and my mum would always go out into the street and scrub the chalk off of the walls. Mum was always such a clean person, and she wouldn't even have the outside of the property looking dirty.

I can still remember the primary school that we went to when we were children, it was a very big red building, and I remember how strict they were over time keeping. But I do not remember an awful lot more about what happened when we went there. I must have been in dreamland!

After a period of time my older sister left the primary school, and she went on to a different school. I know that she became a prefect at this school, and she progressed there very well as she was a lot cleverer than I was as a person.

My mum always sent us to the Sunday school at the church each week, this was the day when we wore our Sunday best clothes (unfortunately this still affects my attitude to clothing today, as I tend to keep everything I buy for best), and on a Friday evening we would go to a place that they called the "Band of Hope" and everyone sang hymns during the course of the evening while we were there!

I also remember that I was a Brownie and later when I was a little bit older, like my sister, I became a Girl Guide, and when I was a little older still I joined something that they called the GTC (the Girls Training Corps). We did a lot of marching when I was in the GTC and I can remember marching in a line with the other girls when there was a big parade in the area of Glasgow where we lived. It seems funny now when I think about it, I really loved marching and I did this on many occasions along with other people, perhaps this was me wanting to perform once again!

Something else that stands out for me was how my mum would leave our home every day for her work (she was the breadwinner in our home). She worked so hard for all of us. On Friday when she got her pay packet, she would take us to the local sweet shop and we would all be given our main weekly treat, a little child's bag of sweets. Our other weekly treat was when she could afford it, she would buy each of us a little cake on a Sunday. I don't know what kind I liked, probably anything as I have a sweet tooth, but I do remember that my older sister loved a little yellow pineapple cake, and she would have one of these each week. Other than this our treats were when our mum made us both mouth-watering Scottish tablet, and boiling sweets for us to eat.

I hope that you can tell from what I am saying here, that I loved and admired my mum, but the thing that sticks out in my mind the most was that my mum was in every way a workaholic. This I am sure was probably necessary in our case as a family. My mum was so tired when she had finished her work that she had no energy left, and we did not do very much together as a family. She didn't have time to read to us at bedtime as some parents did, nor did she have the time to find out how we were doing at school. She was always such a busy person, and everything in our house had to be spotlessly clean at all times. She was so clean as a person, that you could have eaten your food off of our kitchen or living room floor.

It wasn't that mum didn't love us or even want the best for us, but her own life was all about working to support us, and to put the food on the table for us to eat. There weren't many cuddles or much of an expression of love there for us as we grew up. I can remember the one kiss a year that I got from my mum as a child was at the bells at the New Year celebrations. And this was when our mum would walk over and give us a kiss and wish us a happy new year.

I suppose that at this point that I could ask, "What is this thing called love?" I'm not really sure that I know the answer to this any more. But all I can say is that no-one could have done more physically to care for her children than my mother did for her children!

You can also tell from what I am saying here, that as children we were very much left to our own devices. I do remember that on one occasion my mum brought home a police book with a lot of illustrations in it; this was to show us of the many types of dangers faced by the children who took silly risks when they were out playing. And the illustrations in the book that she brought home for us to see that day were certainly a good warning to us.

We did have some good times there in Vicarfield Street when we were young children. It was very much like living in a community where people looked out for each other. During the summertime the ladies who didn't go out to work, would all sit out in the back courts and they would teach us how to knit and sew. This was probably because none of the children who lived there had gardens of their own to play in. The adults who lived there would try to help us and they would share their time with us.

Another highlight for me was when everyone, including the adults would join in a game of rounders. We would play this on the roadside, and everyone joined in the game. And sometimes the ladies would get some long skipping ropes, and we would see how many children could all skip at the same time. We had such a lot of fun with the adults when we were children.

Unlike today, when everyone is chasing enough money to live on, when I was a child the adults did seem to have the time to help us.

The thing that I loved the best at the time though was when we all got together in the back courts, and we all learned to do Scottish country dancing. After we had learned what to do we would then have a special performance of the many things that we had been taught. This was a really exciting evening for everyone who was there at the time, and we would dress up in our Scottish regalia for the performance. This event was mostly performed in the back courts where we lived, and was always organised by the adults who would put on some Scottish music for us to dance to. We would get into our various groups, and we would dance the night away.

At this time of our lives, we were extremely poor in our family, and I can still remember that nearly all of the clothes that I wore were passed down to me from my older sister. For this particular occasion my mum had borrowed a kilt for my older sister from one of our neighbours, but no-one had a kilt that I could wear for the performance. This time though my mother decided to buy a new tartan skirt for me to wear to dance in, but when she got it home to where we lived, my sister wanted to change with me because she also really liked the new skirt. Much to my delight though, my mum asked me which of the two that I wanted to wear. I loved the new red Royal Stewart tartan pleated skirt that she had just brought home, and I said that this was what I wanted to wear for the dance performance.

I have probably never been so proud as I was that day, as we formed into our groups and did our Scottish dancing with me in my red tartan skirt. Ever since then, I have loved music and dancing.

Another thing that I particularly enjoyed as a child was that from time to time we had people who would come and sing in the back courts where we lived. We could even hear them singing their songs in our houses. I can still remember that we had an Irishman who would come along to our back court, and one of the songs that he would usually sing was the lovely song called Danny Boy. I loved hearing him sing this song, he had such a lovely voice, and this will always be a special song to my ears.

Something else I particularly remember was that the people in the street would tell us ghost stories, this was really quite frightening to a little girl, but even so, I am sure that I always believed what they said at the time.

I must have been quite a tomboy, I would play around the area with my friends; we loved to play with balls against the tenement walls; we would also mark the ground with chalk so that we could play games of peever with the other children; and we would climb on anything we could find to jump over, either up and or down, and in many places that I would now consider potentially dangerous for young children. But this was all a part of what we did as young children, and this was probably because none of us had gardens to play in at the time.

Around this time, my mother had a friend in this street, and our mum told us to call her aunty. We all liked this lady and during the time we were living there, we played with her children.

I remember that we all went to a party at her house one evening. My mum already had a husband, my step father, but even then at my young age, I knew that mum was very unhappy being with him, as they used to have terrible rows. I think that this was because he would not go out to work for our family. I can remember my mum sleeping in the bed recess in the kitchen of the house that we lived in. I can still remember putting my arms around my mum each night when we went to our bed. I did this because I believed that I was protecting my mum from her horrible husband! My mother always worked, she would leave our home every day as she always worked her socks off for us as a family.

It was during the time that we were at the party, that mum met another man that she liked. They must have started seeing each other, because after a time they decided to go away together. And with that happening to us as a family, it meant we were suddenly homeless as we had to leave the house that we had been living in. This man was later to become the father of my third sister. He also then became my second step-father, and at the time that this happened to us, they didn't have a home for us to live in.

There were three of us children, and we all went to live in a tent by the seaside, very near to Greenock.

29

Fortunately for us it was the summer time, and we did not have to attend school. I would think that they probably planned it that way, because it was the school holidays. While we were there at the seaside, we spent our days on the beach picking up mussels and shells, and wandering about in the woods. So far as I can remember we only had one tent that we all had to share.

But as was her normal practice, my mum continued to go to her place of work each day while we stayed there playing on the beach. We were only there a short time, when she arrived back one day and she told us that she had found a new home for us to live in!

The house that we moved into was a very large privately owned property. The whole of the house was rented out to a number of other families. As a family, we had a double room apartment in this house. The accommodation that we had was one very large room that had our beds, a table, and some living room furniture in it. The second room which was adjoining was much smaller, and it was a really nice place where we could wash and dress. We shared both the bathroom and the very large kitchen in the house with the other families who lived there.

This house was in the very centre of Glasgow in Scotland. It was in the area that they called Townhead. Another thing that this house had was a very large basement and my mum used to spend her time in there when she had any laundry to do. Prior to this she had to go to a public place that they called a "steamy" to do the family washing. In those days not many people had washing machines in the way that we do today.

When I think of it now, my mum must have found it very difficult there, but I can't remember hearing her complaining once, about either her life, or the circumstances that she was in.

I can remember some of the nice times that we had when we lived in this house. My mum and stepfather had groups of friends around to visit with us, and they would have sing-a-longs that we were all able to join in. Often now when I hear some old songs being played, I can remember hearing my mum singing them. I loved hearing my mum sing, and when they asked me to sing for them, they always asked me to sing 'Beautiful Dreamer'. I'm not so beautiful but sometimes in my life, I am still a dreamer!

The people who lived in this house at that time were really nice, the owner of the house did not live there, but he kept his friendly Alsatian dog there. He was a very gentle dog, and he really loved playing with us children. I think that he was my first real friend in life. I loved playing with Rajah, my new friend, and I spent as much time as I could with him. I really loved him and I believed at the time that he loved me.

I shared such a lot of fun with Rajah my new friend. I so loved playing out in the first garden that we were given to play in. I also had my first bike when we stayed at this address. I could see the primary school that I would be attending from the garden, as the house was in a very elevated position overlooking the school. I used to love this garden, it was the first garden that we had as a family. We would all climb up on the trees and play, and play also with Rajah and any children who were there at the time. So I spent the rest of the summer playing in this lovely garden.

I have just realised that this was not only the first garden, but the only garden that I had to play in as a child!

When the time came to go back to school, I went along to the school that our home and our garden overlooked. The school was called St David's, and I soon realised that I had missed a year of teaching at my previous school, as we had started doing preparations for the qualifying exams (the 11 Plus exams). I had not been taught many of the lessons that they were covering in these exams and this meant that I seemed to be at an immediate disadvantage compared to all of the other children in my classroom. I did however in spite of this, pass my qualifying exams, but only just. I went from this school into the grammar school which was nearby, and this school was called Glasgow City Public. I went in to what was considered to be a "low stream" class of children. While I was there at this school, I took domestic sciences as my subjects. I am sure I learned a lot about housewifery and cooking, sewing and laundering, but I think that I would rather have been learning languages like many of the other children above me did.

I know that the things that I enjoyed doing the most at school were singing, poetry, dancing and art. Most of the other subjects that we were taught, I struggled with. Perhaps it was because the boys in our class at school were very badly behaved, and especially towards our teachers. I have sometimes wondered how I managed to learn anything at all while I was there!

I left this school at around age sixteen because the girl who was my best friend at school was leaving. She went into silver service waiting following in her family's footsteps, and I have not heard anything about her since the day that we left school. The old brain matter still works though, because I can still remember her name and the street that she lived in.

Isn't it sad? Sometimes we get so busy, that we lose touch with the people who meant such a lot to us!

Being in a city school, we had a really good school club, and this was run several evenings a week, I loved going there to the club. I know that we did drama and various other things, but the thing that I always loved the best were the evenings when we did Scottish country dancing.

I can only remember a few things about the school that I attended, but apparently I had had a good Scottish education by the time I was ready to leave there!

When I left school, the first job that I had was working for Collins Bookmakers in Glasgow, Scotland. I was involved in their book-binding section while I was there with them. This came about because when we had school leaving interviews, Collins were looking for young people to go to work there for them. It was suggested to me that I should go to work for them. I tried this but I only lasted for about three months, as I really hated being there. I am sure when I think about it now, that there was nothing wrong with the company, but I know that it just wasn't for me at that time of my life.

One day when I was at home, I was visiting one of the other mums who lived in the same big house that we were living in. I mentioned to her that I was not very happy working at Collins anymore. She suggested to me that I go to a big store in Sauchihall Street and try to get a job there. The store that she sent me to that day was called Muirhead's, and it was one of the large House of Fraser Departmental stores that we had in Glasgow at that time.

When I arrived there, I was directed to this very tall man who was in charge of the store at the time. I should probably have hesitated in talking to him, but I went up to him and I told him that I would like to work there in his store. I think that this may have impressed him, as he gave me a job on the spot. So this was when I went to work in the gown department of the store. And the gown department was run by a very kind and elderly lady by the name of Miss Gilchrist.

Miss Gilchrist ran her department fairly tightly, she was always very kind to me while I worked for her, and at that time she had some lovely ladies working for her. I can particularly remember one of the ladies who worked there, she was called Miss Barclay. She was there when I first started working in the department, I really admired this lady and was really sorry when one day she came in to work, and she told us all that she was leaving to go to work in one of the big department stores in the City of Edinburgh.

I looked up to and admired Miss Barclay, she was such a very kind and an especially nice person towards me during the time that she was there. She was one of the nicest ladies that I have met during my lifetime! I so enjoyed being there in my new job, I started as a junior, and all of the ladies in the department spoiled this very little girl who had just come to work with them. Everyone seemed to like me, as I was willing to do anything that they asked me to do.

During the time that I worked at Muirhead's, my mum and my new stepfather decided to buy a house that had become available very close to where we were living in the big house. It was in a nearby tenement building, and this house was big enough for us as a family. We had a large lounge, and my mum bought some nice furniture for it. She decorated the whole house throughout as she would usually do, and she bought us any furniture that we needed for the house. She also bought us a piano that sadly none of us learned to play. I was really proud of my mum, she seemed to be able to turn her hand to anything, and she really did make us comfortable wherever we were living. She was a very talented woman, and she made our new home a really nice place for us as a family.

It was from this house, our new home, that I also started my singing, most of these were amateur performances, and it was some years later that I started dating your father, while we lived in this house in Grafton Square, Glasgow.

I continued working in Muirhead's gown department for about six years in total. It was really exciting for me, seeing all of the beautiful evening and wedding gowns as they arrived there. We also sold every other outfit that was available on the market at the time. It was a very big department that I worked in, and I always loved unpacking and ironing the lovely gowns which none of the other ladies wanted to do.

One of the sales ladies that I worked with told me that there was a body for everything that we sold in the store. She said that if the customer did not like a pocket, or the collar, or whatever it was that they did not like, that we should just cut it off, this was her way of selling gowns to people.

While I worked there, I was invited out to their family homes to visit with them. I have so many fond memories of them, and the time that I spent with them. As I said the ladies there were so very kind to me, they took this little girl of sixteen and a half years old, and they made my time so very special while I worked there with them.

As I said, I was from a very poor background, everything was a luxury in our home. We did not have many clothes to wear, and even some of the basic food that people ate at the time was in short supply in our family. I can still remember when Miss Gilchrist would send me out on an errand along Sauchihall Street where our store was. While I was walking along, I saw what I thought were rich ladies sitting in tea shops, and they looked as though they were enjoying themselves, as the table that they were sitting at had a lovely assortment of scones and cakes on it. I can remember my thoughts at the time, and I was thinking how lucky they were, and I thought that I would do this when I grew up. I think that this was as near as I got to having an ambition at that time.

Another thing that I found enjoyable was when we had a meeting at the shop and the ladies would ask me to sing for them – I loved singing and entertaining people so I had the opportunity at their meeting to do one of my favourite things.

As you can tell, I loved working there at Muirhead's, it was very exciting for a girl of my age, and I felt so privileged to work there with so many nice people. I can remember during the time I was there, being very interested in what they did with the window dressing and in the publicity department. I did not realise then that I would have been more suited to this kind of work, as I seem to be more artistic as a person, rather than being a clever person.

I was so excited about working there in the store. I can remember the buyer that I worked with correcting me for running everywhere in the store, including up the escalator. Everything was so exciting for me at the time, and she said that she thought that I might run down one of our customers, if I did not stop running about the store.

While I was there, I even got the opportunity to go to my first opera with one of the ladies and her family. I can remember the lady to this very day, she gave me an orange tweedy wool suit to wear for the occasion. Although I should have been acting more like a lady by this time, I was still quite a tomboy at heart. The skirt of the suit was very long and straight. I had not worn any grown up clothing before, and I certainly had not had on a straight skirt before. This was my first grown up outfit, and I was going to the opera, how exciting was that!

I took the suit home, and I tried it on, and I must have liked what I saw in the mirror! I know that I was feeling happy at the time, because I walked out of the door of the tenement building where we lived, and when I reached the top of the stairs what did I do? I did my usual jump down the stairs, all the way from the top to the bottom. And of course you can guess what happened to me that day. I had to suffer the consequences of being so foolish as to jump down all of the eleven steps at the same time. I had quite a bad fall that day, no more than I deserved; but because I felt so stupid, I did not tell anyone what I had done.

But of course, this was not the only stupid thing that I have done in my life, as time will tell!

During the time that I was working at Muirhead's, a young friend that I had in the street where I was living came to work with me in the gown department as our junior member of staff. Although she was a few years younger than I was, we became good friends and as well as the shop work that we did together, we spent our spare time dancing as she was a brilliant Scottish country dancer.

My friend taught me to do the Highland Fling and some of the sword dance (but both are forgotten now). We really enjoyed the time that we spent dancing together in the back courts where we lived. I remember that our dancing teacher held a show locally, and at the time we both performed a Russian dance together on the stage.

We had some really very good times together, we loved our dancing, but sadly our dancing all came to a very quick end. My little friend sadly died when she was still a very young girl of sixteen and a half. And as you can imagine it was never the same for me without her. I will always remember the lovely times that we both shared dancing together in the back courts where we lived. It was such a lot of fun for both of us.

But you know my granddad's name for me was very apt, I was a Stage Struck Fanny; the main thing that I enjoyed in my life was singing; the opportunities that I got in the department store paled into insignificance with the possibility that I may get the opportunity to sing and dance on the stage. Singing was what I loved the most, and this was the thing that I really wanted to do at that time of my life.

I went to the odd talent show as I fancied myself as a budding star, but I didn't get picked out. You can tell from this that I was not good enough, and it was obviously not meant to be; but of course this did not stop me from trying!

I first performed my singing in front of children in our street, I don't know where I learned this song, but I can still remember singing it, it goes like this...

I'm a big girl now;
I want to be treated
like a big girl now,
I'm tired of wearing bobby
socks like kiddies do
I'm tired of going to dances in
my flat heeled shoes
I want the boys to look at me
and shout woo-woo
I'm a big girl now

Anyway as a result of singing this, or not, I was asked to sing at an elderly people's entertainment evening. I can remember that I stood up in this large hall, this was the first time that I had stood on a stage. I didn't even know the words of the song that I was singing properly. I hadn't practiced singing it, but here I was, standing on the stage, and I sang a song that was very popular at the time. I had only heard it a few times before, and it was called "The Indian Love Call'. And I did this in front of a room full of people. And yes, surprisingly they all enjoyed hearing me sing this song even although I did not know all of the words at the time. I suppose all the calling youooo's worked for me at the time!

While I was at this concert, I was asked to join a concert party, so that I could help them to entertain people. This was the first concert party that I was in. We would all travel together in coaches that were hired for the evening, and we would travel to various venues around the Glasgow area to do the different concerts. We went to hospitals, churches and concerts for the elderly and in fact anywhere that wanted someone to entertain them. Apart from one concert that I did at a much later date, all of the other concerts that I did were amateur ones.

It was during this time that I met some people who became very close friends to me for many years after that. The lady was there, because her youngest daughter, who was only four years old at the time, was also in the concert party that I had just joined. This little girl played the accordion, she would walk up on to the stage, and she would be helped on to a chair, and someone would strap the accordion to her. And of course she could play the accordion beautifully, even at that young age. I will never forget when she played "Moon River"; I loved hearing her play this, and this song has been a favourite of mine ever since then.

After this time, the lady and her daughter became very close friends of mine. I have many fond memories of the times that we would go out to concerts together. I also had the opportunity to spend a lot of my spare time with them as a family, as from then on, I was a regular visitor to their home, and we all shared many good times together.

It turned out that my new friend's daughter was having singing lessons from a singing teacher in Glasgow. And when I got to know her better, she asked me to come along to one of the singing lessons with her, as she wanted the singing teacher to hear me sing. So I went there to the studio with them one evening. The teacher took some music, she played the piano for me, and she liked my voice so much that she said that she wanted to train me. She was a very experienced teacher who had previously trained people who were professional singers. By now I was already a young adult, but because I did not have a lot of money, she said that she would charge me only the juvenile rate for the training. I started then to have a weekly lesson with her, and I paid for these lessons with the money that I had left after paying my mum for my keep.

Anyway, you can tell that this singing teacher was very dedicated to her work, as well as the time I spent with her on my singing lessons, and in spite of the fact that she was very much older than I was at the time, we would spend most of the rest of the evening after my lesson together. During these evenings we would debate on various subjects that we enjoyed talking about. We both became very good friends, and when she later started up a concert party herself, I was able to join this and sing for her there!

I seemed to be making a lot of friends in Glasgow at that time. Many of the friends that I made worked with

41

me at Muirhead's, and most of them were a lot older than me, as some of them had been working there all of their lives. But there was one lady that I became particularly friendly with, she was an elderly lady at this time, and she was a Baptist. Like me she also enjoyed singing, and I would often go to her home after work. She would play the organ, and I would sing to the music that she played. We learned to harmonise together, and we became very good at this. I would meet with her each Sunday, and I would go with her to the Baptist church that she attended. And each Saturday evening we would go together to the Tent Hall in Glasgow, and we would harmonise to the music, and sing our hearts out there.

At this time, I was also having the opportunity to sing solos in quite a number of churches around the Glasgow area. But I was never good enough to sing in the very large Tent Hall that my friend and I went to on Saturdays. I was just sixteen and a half years old when I committed my life to God by accepting Jesus as my saviour.

So for a number of years, I went out singing at every opportunity that I got. I even sang a song in the famous Princess Street Gardens in Edinburgh. I couldn't have been a complete failure to get this opportunity!

During all of this time our home was in Grafton Square in Glasgow. Things seemed to continue okay for us at home, as at this time we seemed to have something akin to a normal family life. My older sister also had a good job, as she had done really well at her school.

We must have been becoming just a little bit better off as a family, because my older sister and I were both working, and as a result of this, we were able to put some small amounts of money into the home budget, to help my mum with the housekeeping. What a relief that must have been for her, as she had really struggled to bring us up!

It wasn't long though before we had the news that my older sister had met a really nice man in our local community, and they started dating together. He was a really nice person, and my sister really loved the times that she would go over and stay at his mum's house. She obviously did this for some time, and then they announced to us all that they were going to be married. I was a bridesmaid at the wedding which we all enjoyed, and as you all know, because you met them later, they had a long and successful marriage together, and they have three lovely daughters, whom I know you have all met.

My sister's wedding was now over, everything had gone well on the day, and this meant that we were then one person less at home. Gradually things were getting settled for us as a family again, when suddenly my mum came in one day and very reluctantly and rather sheepishly announced to us that she was going to have another baby. Now my mum was very embarrassed about this, her daughters were all growing up, one had just got married, and here she was announcing to us that she was having another baby. And when she told us about this my mum was then forty-six years of age. But in spite of my mum's age at the time, everything seemed just normal for her and for the baby.

Yes, the day finally came, and she went in to the local hospital and gave birth to a little daughter. I can remember visiting my mum in the hospital just after she had given birth to my new sister. My mum must have

43

been so pleased that her new baby was healthy and normal, in spite of my mum's age at the time.

I know that many years later my mum must have been so very pleased that she had this late daughter, this daughter was the one who looked after her, both in her old age and later when she was in a nursing home. My mum deserved something good to happen to her; she had a really hard life. And her youngest daughter looked after her really well until the day came when she sadly left this earth!

Just after the birth of our new sister, we had such a lot of fun with her in our family. My younger sister who had always been ill and who had recently had a bad accident as a young woman was asked by mum if she would look after the new baby during the day. This was so that my mum could go back out to work again, because she needed to support us. It was actually rather amazing to all of us, that our mum completely recovered after such a late birth.

After I lost my own daughters, I wrote to my mum and I told her how much I appreciated everything that she had done for us as children, but she never discussed this with me. She was just so private about her life!

Anyway as it turned out, we all loved this little new addition to our family, she was such a lovely little thing, and we all loved her from the moment that she arrived. I know that I really enjoyed all of the long walks that I took her to the parks, when she was still a baby in her pram.

So our home life began to be quite normal for us once again, and we all got on with our lives and with the things that we had to do. I had loved the times that my friend and I spent when we were practicing our dancing in the back courts near to where we lived. I am sure that she was a great influence in getting me to try different types of dancing, as she was such a talented dancer. We had started tap dancing as well as the Scottish country dancing, and so dancing became another of my favourite things.

It won't be a surprise to you, when I tell you that we went on a family night out to the Locarno ballroom in Glasgow. I went with my mum and the current stepfather. At the time I was there I did my first session of ballroom dancing, and I realised then that I loved this type of dancing, as well as all of the others that I had tried. It is not that I am particularly good, as I am just a social dancer, but I must admit to enjoying every minute of the time that I spend when I dance.

It was very soon after this occasion at the Locarno that one of the ladies that I worked with at Muirhead's came in one day, and she said that her husband, a policeman, could get me free passes into the Dennistoun Palais on Wednesday evenings. She asked me if I would like to have these tickets, and of course I jumped at the chance, as I could spend these evenings doing one of my favourite things, and for free.

And so to add to all of my other activities, I started to go regularly to the Dennistoun Palais to a ballroom dance on a Wednesday evening. So this then was my routine as a young woman, singing lessons once a week, concert party work, going to church on Sundays and often doing the special music when I was asked to. I was still visiting my friend who played the organ in her home, and visiting

45

the home of the other friends that I had made at the first concert party that I had joined.

Yes, I was really enjoying being a young adult. I didn't do anything way out like they do today, I hadn't even heard of drugs or raves. I wasn't yet too interested in clothes or boys. I didn't have much money either, but what I had, I spent on doing the two things that I loved the best.

And of course my favourite things were singing and dancing!

It was because of my love of dancing, that I decided to go along to some of the other lovely ballrooms that they had in the Glasgow area at that time. I tried several of them, and the other one that I particularly liked and enjoyed going to was the Majestic Ballroom, and this one was fairly near to where I lived in the Centre of Glasgow.

From this time onwards, my favourite venue for a Saturday evening was the Majestic ballroom. Just like many of the other ballrooms in Glasgow, it had a very large and beautiful dance floor for everyone, and it was always full of music and laughter. I also found out that I was meeting some nice people there, and it was here that I was to meet the man who was to become your father and my first love!

During the day I was still working in the gown department at Muirhead's. I worked in this store for about six years in total, and I got to know the ladies who worked there really well during the time that I was there. I didn't even have any thoughts about leaving there, until one day when I went upstairs with the alterations from our gown department, and the lady who was the head of the alteration department told me of a position that had become available at her daughter's employers; and at the time she asked me if I would be interested in the job. As I said, I hadn't thought to leave my place of work, but at the time, this seemed to be too good an opportunity for me to miss. So I decided there and then that I would go to this company for an interview. I had not worked in an office before, but surprise, surprise, the company offered me the position that very day, and of course I was very excited at the prospect of this new job. And as I could see it then, another benefit to me was that I would have every Saturday to myself.

Miss Gilchrist, the buyer of the department, did everything that she could to try to persuade me to continue working for her, she said that she had wanted to train me as a buyer, or even as a model, but nothing that she said to me could persuade me to stay there. She asked the store manager to speak to me about it, but by this time I realised that I would be better off to make the move from there. I also had the added bonus of not having to work all day on a Saturday. And so I continued with my plans, I worked my notice, and I left the store.

After working in a large department store for so long, I found it quite difficult to change and get myself used to working in an office. My job for my new employer was to do all of the stock control for them.

The company supplied meat to various companies all around the Glasgow area, and I had the job of keeping accurate figures for them. These figures showed the daily losses in meat that each of the drivers had when they came back in the evenings from their deliveries. All of these figures were done manually on hand written sheets of paper, as this was before the time that we all had computers and spreadsheets to use. As you can imagine, there were always discrepancies, and the drivers had to explain to the management how they managed to mysteriously lose some of their stock.

Because I was good at the fine detail that they required, I did quite well in this new position, and I worked for this company for some time, and I continued to work there for them, until your father had finished university, and we were ready to start our new life together in England.

With my sister and my aunt in Cardross

Chapter 2
Meeting Your Father

The first time that I met your father, I was out enjoying myself at one of my favourite activities, because when we met up, I was enjoying an evening out at the Majestic Ballroom in Glasgow. And as you know by now, dancing was one of my favourite things, and it had been since we did the Scottish country dancing in the back courts where we lived in Govan. At the time that I met your dad, I didn't have any serious thoughts about boyfriends, because after an unusual childhood I had grown up to enjoy so many of the things that I did as a young woman.

But on this particular night, I was invited to dance by this rather nice, and as I thought at the time, handsome young man. I suppose that I was flattered that evening as we danced around the floor as he seemed to enjoy dancing with me, and he also seemed to enjoy my company as well.

And yes, this young man was your father!

And yes, we continued dancing together throughout the whole of the evening, and when the evening came to a close, and because we had enjoyed ourselves so much, we arranged to meet there again the following Saturday. As I said, I wasn't too serious about meeting anyone at that time of my life; I had not even thought of it, as at the time I was happy doing the things that I already loved and enjoyed. I was still having my singing lesson once a week, and I was in several concert parties. In addition to this I was doing the special music for various churches at this time. Life seemed good to me, and having a serious friendship was not on my agenda.

I know that around this time, that I had also arranged to meet up with another young man, and I had let him down by not turning up at the meeting place, and this was because I did not want to get involved with anyone.

But as had become my habit, I did go to the Majestic the following Saturday, and very much to my surprise your father turned up there again, he told me that he hoped to meet me there again. So here we were, once again spending yet another evening together. We laughed, and we danced the night away, and we really enjoyed the time that we spent together. And as it turned out, this man that I was dancing with was your father, and the person who would feature quite a lot in my future from this time onwards.

I later found out from him that he was studying at the time for a degree at Glasgow University. I think that at the time that we met, that he had only just started this course, as he was only eighteen at the time that we met. Anyway he said that he was hoping to have a good future ahead of him. Little did we know then, or could we even have guessed, what the future was going to bring to both of us!

Your father told me that he lived with his parents and one of his sisters in a place called Bellsmyre in Dumbartonshire.

Now I knew a bit about Dumbartonshire, but not Bellsmyre. Incidentally though the place that he lived with his parents and his sister was only about four miles away from where my relatives lived, and where my mother was brought up, as it was about fourteen miles outside of Glasgow. So after we socialised that evening, and because we seemed to get on quite well, we arranged to meet at the Majestic Ballroom the following week.

We continued meeting each other from this time on, and we always danced the night away on these occasions. And because we got on so well with each other, and also because we enjoyed each other's company, we decided to continue seeing each other. And it was from this time onwards that we started to date each other regularly. This was the beginning of what could, and should have been an exciting future for both of us!

And as the song says; we were "getting to know you, you are precisely my cup of tea", and so it was from this time on, that we continued to see each other. And we became each other's best friend, or at least I thought that we did. And as these things happen, when you continue seeing someone that you are attracted to, you fall in love!

But alas as time will tell, this was not to be!

So from this time on, we spent as much time as we possibly could together, your father had grown up in a musical family, and he could also sing fairly well. He seemed to really enjoy coming with me to my singing lesson, and enjoy the time that we spent with my singing teacher.

At this time your father had a bantam motor bike, and we would drive into the countryside on this. We would take a picnic with us when we went up the hills around

Loch Lomond and we also went Balloch and walked by the loch on some lovely summer days. It is so lovely there at Balloch and in the hills around Loch Lomond, and we spent quite a lot of our time together in this area.

At the time that we started our dating, your dad had a jacket that he wore when he was on his motorbike. You will all probably think that this is stupid, but do remember that we were both very young at the time. We called this jacket rusty, it was a deep blue colour with a creamy fur collar, and I haven't seen one quite like it since then. Anyway he would ask me to put my arms around rusty (so that I wouldn't fall off of the motorbike of course), it was great fun for us, and we both loved the times when we went out on his motorbike together, as this was our only means of transport at the time.

So yes we became inseparable as a couple, and we went everywhere we possibly could together.

And this is how the scene was set for our future together. A naive girl and as I found out later a bullying and controlling young man!

Your father told me that he was born in Hessle in Hull, and when he was about three years old his parents decided to move to Scotland. They arrived there in the West coast of Scotland in Dumbartonshire, and I think that they struggled there for quite a bit in unsuitable accommodation. After they lived in the area for some time, they moved into a really nice council house in a little housing estate called Bellsmyre. This is like a small district very near to the town of Dumbarton. It was in this area that your father went to school, and where he spent his younger days.

I know that he liked living there when he was a young child, he told me so many stories of the times that he spent in that area. I remember he told me that he had once gone out in the middle of the night to some farm fields that were near to his home. It was a very dark night, and as he walked along he suddenly heard the sound of footsteps following him, and at the time he was quite worried as every time he stopped, the footsteps also stopped. Anyway he began to get quite concerned, but he thought at the time that it would be better if he were to continue walking. He was hoping that he would get away from the footsteps, when suddenly he saw the outline of a horse in the distance in front of him. It was the horse that was following him all of the time, and there was nothing for him to worry about after all.

I think that there was also a special girl for him at school, he walked her home each day and carried her school books home for her.

There is no reason that I can think of, for me to think that he had anything unusual happen to him as a young child. He seemed to me to have a normal family life, and he had two lovely parents. I particularly loved his dad, as he became like a father figure to me. You know that I had not had a dad of my own as I had grown up, and your grandfather always treated me like one of his own daughters. Your father had two sisters, one who was ten years older than he was, and she was already married when I met him. He also had one younger sister, and she was really like a very young child, she was very small, and she was a Down Syndrome child.

Your father's older sister was such a nice and kind lady! I really came to love her very much over the years

54

that I knew her. She was always very hospitable to me any time that we met, and we used to spend a lot of our time with both his sister and her husband. Her husband was a Church of Scotland minister at this time!

Your father's background was just the same as it was for a lot of people in those days, as they were not well off as a family. And yet his parents were managing to support your dad while he was at the university. Your grandfather did as most dads do, they go out to earn a living, and his mum was an at home housewife, and they both enjoyed the nice and modest home that they all shared together.

The person in the house though, who seemed to be the main driving force was his mum, as she controlled the day to day running of things in the home. In those days women seemed to be stay at home housewives, as most ladies did not go out to work at that time. She was very ambitious for her son, and she planned for him to do well, both at school and later at the university.

I expect that your father had a much better home life than I had as a child. He was fortunate to have two parents pulling together, and trying to do their best for their family. I know though that it was particularly hard for his mum, as his younger sister had to be constantly looked after, and this must have been quite a strain on all of them.

As I mentioned, your father's older sister was married when we met, and at the time I met him they were living in a tiny little village between Glasgow and Edinburgh called Longriggend. They lived in a church house that was very big, and it was called a "manse" in Scotland, I do not know what they call these houses in

England, but "manse" was what they were called in Scotland.

We spent much of our time and our courtship in their home, both with them, and their constant stream of visiting friends and family. You could always be sure of a good Scottish welcome when you visited them there.

I obviously don't know about how he is now, but in those days your father was really good company; he had a really good sense of humour; he was attractive to me; and fun to be with. He became my closest friend and companion. It is very hard to find such pals as I thought that we were at that time!

During the early years when we were getting to know each other, we spent a lot of our time with his parents at their home. Your father had passed his school exams and he had already started at Glasgow University by the time that we met. His mother was very keen that he should do really well in his studies at the university, and she encouraged him in every way that she could.

His mum was a bit disappointed that her daughter had not done better for herself. She didn't think that a Church of Scotland Minister was the best possible husband that she could have had. Especially as her son-in law had a good professional qualification before he had his calling into the ministry. So you can see from the attitude that she had, that she obviously wanted her family to do well for themselves. But you know, his sister's husband was a very dedicated person, in his work he did a perfectly wonderful job of looking after his flock, as well as everyone else that he came into contact with. These two people together were very special people, full of love and service, and they also worked very well as a couple, as they really loved each other.

But even although we were having an enjoyable time getting to know each other, we had to remember that at this time your father was studying for a BSc degree at Glasgow University, and it was very important for him to have sufficient time in his preparation work for his course. So apart from special days and holidays, I would travel each Sunday to his family home, so that we could at least have some time together, while he was getting on with his course work. So this became the norm for us, he would stay at home at the weekend, and I would travel down there to where they lived in Bellsmyre, because by doing this, we could spend some time both together and of course with his family.

Your father's younger sister was a very small, and a rather weak little girl, as she was ill with tuberculosis nearly all of the time that I knew her. She was such a sweet little child, and she totally relied on other people to help her. She seemed to like it when I went over there to visit, and while your dad was studying, I was able to go to her bedroom and sit with her. I think that your grandmother was really pleased for me to spend this time with her on these evenings, as it must have been really hard for her to keep looking after her daughter, and to give her the constant care that she needed.

At the beginning of our friendship, your grandmother always made me feel very welcome there at their home. It was really important to her that your dad spend as much time as he could in preparation for his exams, as he was studying at the time for a degree in Electrical Engineering at the university. His mother was the real driving force in this family, and she was happy for me to spend my time with them, as she knew that her son had to put the study time in to be able to get his degree. His mother did not go out to work, but she was a good housewife and she looked after her family very well. At the time that I met her she always made us all nice sandwiches for lunch, and then a nice cooked dinner in the evening, which we all enjoyed. Very often when I was there, your grandmother's brother would travel over from Glasgow where he lived in a hotel, and he would join us all for Sunday lunch.

I can remember that I had my first birthday cake in their house, it was made by your grandmother, and it was to celebrate my 21st birthday. We all had a lovely meal and then the cake was brought in, and everyone was toasting me. She really did make me feel like a part of the family!

Your grandfather, your dad's father was a really lovely and a very kind man, he loved a simple life, and his home and family. He kept a well-stocked garden that was always very nice, as he really enjoyed working in his very well kept garden. He was there every Sunday tending the garden, and enjoying his time away from his work. Your grandfather was very musically talented, and he had a most lovely baritone voice.

I loved the times I spent with them, we didn't have such strong family bonds in my family, even although my mum did her best for us, she was always working, and family life was very basic in our home. And it was probably because of this, that I really enjoyed being part of this family. Their house was an ordinary semi-detached house with three bedrooms. His mother kept it clean and tidy, but it was a very basic home. Most people during that time lived in very modest circumstances, and their family were no exception to this. His father was an ordinary hard working man, and he did what he could to support his wife and family. They had to sacrifice quite a lot as a couple to put your father through university.

Other things changed for me at this time, as they always do when you meet someone, and instead of going to the Baptist church with my friend Miss Black in Glasgow, we together started to attend one in Dumbarton on a Sunday. Dumbarton is a small town just a short distance from where your father lived in Bellsmyre. And in the nice weather if we had time, we would go out for a drive on your dad's motorbike. We would go into the hills around Loch Lomond, and we would sometimes go over to the Balloch area, as this was only a short bike ride from their home.

I can still remember the time that we were out walking somewhere in Balloch and near to Loch Lomond, and we had to jump over a stream to get to the other side. It was quite a distance and your father made it over all right. But silly me; I think that I changed my mind about jumping on the way across, and I landed right in the middle of the stream! And at the time I got rather wet. Have you heard of this: 'he who hesitates is lost', well in this case, it was she who hesitates is lost!

Anyway we always enjoyed ourselves, it is so very beautiful around that area, and we had some really good times while we were there. We both loved the area, and we were happy and enjoying the lovely summer weather, and of course really enjoying each other's company.

Gradually I got to know your grandparents quite well, and they both treated me a bit like a member of the family. And it was because things were going so well for us, that after a couple of years we decided to get engaged to be married. No-one in either of our families seemed to object to this at the time.

I can even remember the time that both your grandfather, and another man who was a tenor, sang with me in the Bellsmyre church. Your grandfather had an especially nice baritone voice, and we all sang very well together on that occasion. Your grandfather always treated me like a daughter from the very first moment that we met each other, and he had one of the nicest male voices that I have ever heard at any time in my life!

Your grandfather and his brother had at some time in the past been professional musicians, they had met and married two sisters who were also musicians. Your grandmother played the piano, your grandfather the trumpet, your aunt and uncle played in the BBC orchestra some time before I met them. Your father's older sister also played the piano, and of course music was one of my most favourite things! When we went to your dad's sister's house in Longriggend, we had some lovely times there. I remember many occasions when we would all gather around the piano and sing. I really loved the times that I spent with them as a family.

One of the songs that we would sing as we gathered around the piano at the manse was this one, and I have loved it ever since:

When you come to the end of a perfect day
And you sit alone with your thoughts
When the chimes ring out with a carol gay
For the joy that the day has brought
For memory has painted that perfect day
In colours that never fade
And you find at the end of a perfect day
The joy of a friend you've made.

You know when we sang this, I probably thought that life was wonderful, this song had such a lot of meaning to my mind, but I am afraid that the days ahead did not turn out to be as perfect as the sentiments in the song suggest. Not for me anyway!

But getting back to the story, and you can probably tell, I particularly loved being with your dad's sister, as we both had a really good relationship. Your father's sister was such an amazing and very kind person, she always treated me like a sister, and made me very welcome in her home. She was married and her husband was a dedicated minister, who did whatever he could to help the people in his charge in the local community where they lived. And I thought when we were there with them at the manse, that life had become pretty near perfect, for me anyway!

Your father and I both loved his Bantam motor bike, we usually travelled everywhere on this. We would travel to be with his sister and her husband as often as we could, as we both loved spending our time with them. Christmas, New Year, birthdays, in fact any time was a special occasion to be enjoyed in their home. We spent a lot of our courtship in their home. They were always so welcoming to us, and we spent many good times around their dining room table, with their very many visitors.

There was always a warm welcome there for anyone who went there, as they were people who loved entertaining other people. This was because your father's brother-in-law had the job of looking after and caring for people, and he couldn't have done more for the people that he knew. Their house was very cold in winter, as many Scottish houses seemed to be at that time, but in spite of the fact that they didn't have any central heating, you could always be sure of a warm welcome for anyone who visited them.

As a minister's wife your aunt would spend a lot of her time growing vegetables for her guests to enjoy, and she loved baking and cooking, her table was always full of goodies that she had made. We sat down around the table for each meal, breakfast, eleven o'clock break, we had a very nice lunch, and then a lovely spread for tea, and later if you could believe it, and eat any more, she would spread out another table of goodies for everyone who was there for supper. Money was in short supply in their house, but I can remember someone saying once, that your aunt could make a dinner out of an 'Oxo' cube. It really was like the story of the five loaves and fishes from the Bible when you were there!

Your father's older sister will always have a very special place in my heart! Nothing was ever too much for her to do for anyone!

Sometimes when we were there, I was asked to sing for the special music at their church. And of course I always loved doing this, and it was so nice to be asked to do it. And when we sang at their home around the piano, we all did our various parts, and I know that this made a joyful noise, and it was enjoyed by all of us. As I said before, one of the songs that we sang there was "When you come to the end of a perfect day", I think that this was a special song for them as well as for me.

They always had lots of guests in their homes, both from the family and the church. When we were there, we would all sit around the dining room table sharing meals, and then debating it seemed for many hours, on the various topics that were relevant at the time. The subjects were things that were happening both in the parish, and the church, and the world in general. Everyone had their say, and this was always a very enjoyable and fun time for everyone. You can tell from what I am saying here, that I really felt a part of this family, even before we were married!

I spent some years getting to know your dad and his family, it was fairly obvious before we married that your dad was quite a controlling person. But you know what it is when you think that you love someone, your mind plays tricks on you, and you think that your love can overcome anything, and of course everything. Anyway I am sure that I thought a bit like this at the time!

Now during each summer break from university, your dad would go away for some work experience, and for the one prior to his final year at the University, he was asked to go to Edinburgh to have some further training and work experience. So this was to be the last summer break, before the preparation for his degree exams. He spent this particular year at a company based somewhere around the Edinburgh area. During the time that he was there, he stayed in a lodging room, in the City of Edinburgh itself.

At this time, I was still in Glasgow working in my job at Muirhead's, but because we wanted to see each other during the week, your dad asked me to travel by train to spend some time with him a couple of evenings a week in Edinburgh. So I did this, I travelled there by train after finishing my work at the shop two of the evenings each week. We really enjoyed all the good things that Edinburgh offers to young people. We spent our time walking around the city, the weather was so lovely that year, and we both enjoyed spending our time there. We walked in the park in the lovely Princess Street gardens, this was especially nice for me, as it brought back the memories of seeing my mum sitting there in the band stand, and listening to me singing on the stage a short time before.

We were already engaged to be married at this time, so it will not be a complete surprise for you to hear, that during one of my visits to the city of Edinburgh was when we started to discuss when we should get married. We had been engaged for a couple of years by this time, and it was only a question of when we would go ahead with this. Perhaps the subject came up because we were having such a nice time there, it is such a wonderful place to be. It was summertime, we were happy together, the weather was lovely and the subject was probably always on the back of our minds.

We both loved it there in Edinburgh, it is a cold and windy place in the winter, but in the summertime it is a fantastic and fun place to be, and it is always brimming with life, and things for people to do and enjoy. I have yet to meet the person who did not like the time that they spent in Edinburgh!

So it was during one of these weeks when we were in Edinburgh, that we made the decision to go ahead with our wedding plans, even although we knew that your father still had his final year to do at the university. And of course as a result of this, we went home and announced it to both of our families. Now everyone in both of our families felt as happy as we were about this, we had been engaged for some time, and it was only a question of when for us. But unfortunately we hit what was a major snag; your grandmother on your father's side did not want us to get married. This was in spite of the fact that we were already engaged and happy together.

In actual fact she was rather furious about this idea that we had, apparently she hoped we would not get married then, as she thought that her clever son should finish university and help to support their family.

When I look back now, I can think that perhaps she was right in thinking this, it was just before your dad's final year at the university, and we could have picked a better time to do this. Your dad would not be able to get a good job and support their family, if we were to get married. But you know, we were young, and perhaps in this case rather foolish, we thought that we were in love, and by this time we were very excited about the idea of being together all of the time, at least I know that I was thinking this!

But at the time, in spite of your grandmother's objections, we decided that we would continue with our plans to marry, and I know that it must have been a bit of a blow to her at the time. But we knew that she wouldn't have been happy, even if we had waited until your father had finished his studies, and so we continued planning our wedding.

Neither of us had very much money at this time of our lives, but we managed to scrape together enough money to buy a wedding dress for me, we bought the cake, we organised the hall for the reception, decided on the flowers, and in fact we did all of the things that you do when you are getting married.

As I didn't have a father to ask to give me away, I thought that my nice grandfather would do this for me. I took a trip to Cardross (by this time my grandmother was no longer with us), and I asked my grandfather to give me away. He didn't want to do this, and he suggested that my uncle who lived in Helensborough would be happy to do this for me. I later asked my uncle who said that he was very happy to give me away that day!

So the day of the wedding arrived, and as you would expect, all of us were on a high that day except the one person, your grandmother was adamant that she would not attend our wedding. We sent a car to collect her, but she would not get into the car and she refused 'point blank' to have anything at all to do with our wedding. Afterwards several family members tried hard to persuade her to come and they failed, and we decided to go ahead with the wedding without her.

We were married that day, and after the wedding all of our guests went to a restaurant that was in Dumbarton town centre, and we had a lovely tea there. So now we were a married couple with the whole of our future ahead of us.

Our wedding was a very small one, but of course, at the time I thought that it was "my lovely day", and "the day I shall remember til the day I'm dying!"

So we started out our married life on that day, most of the people who came to the wedding enjoyed our wedding day. The only thing that made it rather sad for everyone who was involved, was that the one main person who should have been there, your grandmother, would not attend the wedding, and she would not give us her blessing.

And you know from that day onwards she was awkward with us, we always knew that she disapproved of us getting married. It also made things so very sad in the family after this happened, as she became very angry and aggressive over so many other issues that were happening in the family from that day.

After our wedding day was over, the guests all left and went on their various ways home again. We travelled from Dumbarton to the Covenanters Inn in Aberfoyle for the weekend on our honeymoon. This was all that we could afford at the time, but we had a really enjoyable time there, as when we arrived at the inn there was another wedding party there.

We had a lovely time while we were there as we got to know the couple who had also just got married that day. We enjoyed the lovely log fire that they had at the inn, we enjoyed a really nice meal, and later we were able to join in the dancing that they were having that evening at the inn.

The following day we all four of us went out together for a walk, and so the weekend was a great success, and very happy for all of us.

And we had made some new friends!

My mother (left) with my aunt

Chapter 3
A Loving Husband or a Bully?

And so this was the way we started our married life. We had the full support of everyone in our families, but a lot of opposition from the one person that your father was probably the closest to, his mother. This wasn't the beginning that we had hoped for, but from the time we announced our wedding plans, your grandmother seemed to set her mind against us.

And this was what we had to deal with, right from the very moment that we announced our plans to marry. And it was from that day onwards that your grandmother started to cause problems for all of us within the immediate family. And in the circumstances what could anyone do? Of course we all carried on as normally as we could. We all hoped that one day in the future, that she would change her mind, and accept that we were now married. This then was the beginning of our life together, and how our married life started.

It is probably true, that you do not know someone properly until you have tried to live with them. Unlike today, in our current society, many couples choose to spend time getting to know each other and also living together before they get married; we did not live together until after our wedding day. And of course, it is only when you do live under the same roof together, that you find out the faults and failings that you both have. And of course we were no exception to this. Until our wedding took place, I was still living at home with my family in Glasgow, and your father was living at home with his parents and his sister in Bellsmyre, Dumbartonshire.

Before our big day we found ourselves some lodgings to rent for the start of our marriage. The accommodation was a room in a tenement building, and this room was where we were to spend the beginning part of our marriage. The room was located very near to the university, and we chose it because we needed to give your dad the maximum time to study, and so that he did not have to spend a lot of time each day travelling to the university. We knew that your father's exams would be held at the university the following spring, and that they would be the final exams that he would have to take. And we also knew that if he passed them, he would have his long awaited degree.

And so this was the reason that we chose this place for the start our married life!

But as you can imagine, once we had moved in to our new lodgings, and we came down to earth once again, our lives started to change quite dramatically from then on out. Many things were now very different for both of us, and we had to get used to a completely new arrangement of living.

The room where we were going to live was in one of Glasgow's large tenement buildings. It was an old building, and the room that we had was a little bit like a studio flat today. It was like living open plan, with everything in the one room. Things were a lot harder for folk in those days, and we were very grateful to be there. It wasn't modern, but it had everything that we needed, and it was really very adequate for our needs. It had a bed, chairs, table, wardrobe, chest of drawers etc., and in fact everything that we needed at that time.

We shared the bathroom and the kitchen facilities with both the landlady and the other tenants who lived there. Unfortunately for us, the landlady did not like her tenants using her kitchen, never mind them cooking there. As a result of this, I didn't do much cooking while we lived there, and that's perhaps the reason why I don't seem to spend a lot of time cooking today. I can't think of what we ate during the time that we were there, we must have lived on convenience foods, but we did survive, even although our meals were rather fragmented at the time.

Anyway somehow we managed to live there, we started off quite happily, in spite of the restrictions that neither of us had been used to. After all, we were living in someone else's house, and the lady who owned it was a fairly strict person. Anyway it was necessary for us to settle down there, and get used to it. We both knew that it was for a short time, and only until your father had finished his studies; we knew that we would be moving from there again, sometime in the future.

So from that time on, it was down to the nitty-gritty of our lives! Your dad was going each day to the university for his studies, and I was getting up each morning and heading off to my place of work, as at that time I was supporting both of us. Because we were both busy working, the time soon slipped away, and it didn't seem long until it was the first break and our trip to Longriggend for the Christmas holidays. We always loved it there, and we started looking forward to sharing both Christmas and the New Year holidays with your dad's sister and her husband, and the other members of our family.

We enjoyed all the fun of the Christmas holidays; it was lovely seeing everyone and having such a happy time. But the holidays were soon over and it wasn't long before we were heading back to Glasgow for your father's final year at the university. What a lovely time we had had with everyone, we were feeling happy and rested and ready to face the days that lay ahead of us with its many challenges!

But the days passed by, and we soon started to approach spring, and the time of your father's final exams at the university. But your dad said then that he was worried about taking the exams at that time. He said that because he really wanted to get the honours part of the degree, that he should postpone his exams until the autumn. So after discussing this with me, he told the university that he was going to postpone his final exams and take them in the autumn of that year.

This change to our plans also meant that we would be living in our apartment during the summer, and also up until the time of his exams in the autumn.

It was shortly after this time however, that your father said that he was having a problem with our landlady. Your father said to me that he wasn't happy, because the landlady seemed to be checking up on our movements!

Now it was perhaps because the evenings were lighter that your dad had noticed this, or perhaps she usually did this to the people who were living in her house. But your father really did not like this, and he was always bugged about it from that time on. Now perhaps at the time, we should have even considered that she was just another elderly and lonely person, and that she had nothing else to do with her time. But at this time of our lives, we were both young, and you know what, all we could see was what was happening to us!

At the time that this was happening, I was going out to work each day, as I needed to support us. So at the time I wasn't really bothered about this, but I had to admit that it was badly affecting your dad. He said that our landlady was spying on us, and that she was very nosy. He was so unhappy about it, that your dad started to actively try to find out why; he wanted to know what she was up to! You know, I jokingly feel like adding here, that perhaps she belonged to the KGB, but this is not really a joke book!

So anyway we continued living there in her house. I thought that we would have to get used to whatever it was that was happening there, including the fact that the landlady seemed to be constantly checking up on our movements.

Now one of the times when I came home from my work, your dad told me that our landlady had also started to go through our personal papers after we had left home. Now at that time of my life, I did not have anything to be secretive about, so I wasn't bothered about this. But I knew that this was again having a bad effect on your father, and because this was happening your father told me that he had decided that he was going to start to set traps for her.

So we went through our room, and he showed me all of the things that he was doing. He started putting a piece of paper behind our room door, and if it wasn't where we left it when we arrived back, we would know that she had been in to our room. He also decided to put papers in drawers and in wardrobes to see if they had fallen to the floor, and etc., and this was all of the way through our room. I think that this is quite funny now, especially when I realise that at the time that this was happening, we could have had a private box to put our papers in, but we were both young, and we hadn't even thought of this!

As you will realise, I don't think that I was personally taking this very seriously, and at the time that this was happening, I even thought that it was rather strange behaviour on our part. I was used to living in a house with other family members, and in any case, at that time of my life, I did not have anything that I needed to hide from anyone. But I went along with what your dad wanted, as he seemed to be rather uncomfortable about it all. So every time we left the room, we went through the same procedure, all of the traps were set, both behind the room door, in wardrobes and cupboard doors etc., and all of these were set each time we left there by your father.

Isn't life exciting? I am being facetious as you will realise, but yes it seemed to be true, she was actually watching us each time that we left there. Neither of us knew why, but as your dad said, every time we left the house to go anywhere, she was there at the window watching us, and of course each time that we went out,

74

when I looked up, there she was looking down on us from above.

This continued for some time, and when we arrived home from anywhere, we would creep into our room, we would check to see if she had been in our room. You could always tell if the paper had been moved that your dad had placed behind the room door when we left. If she had been in, he would then check all of the cupboards, drawers and etc., to see if she had touched anything.

Thinking about this now, we should perhaps have moved on from there, but as it happened, we continued to live there, and it was always a problem from then on. But at the time and because it was easier for us, we decided to stay there in that situation. It was only going to be some months before your father could take his degree examinations, and we knew that after this everything would get easier for us.

As I said, I thought at the time that your father's behaviour was rather strange. I am sure that he didn't ask her why she was watching us? But I know that I continued to go along with whatever your dad wanted to do. By this time in our marriage, I was getting used to doing whatever your dad wanted to do. Every time that we went out of the house, we would stand there looking up at the window, so that she knew, that we knew, that she was watching us.

And so the intrigue continued!

As you know, I went out to work each day, this was to support us and give your dad the maximum time to spend in his final year of studies. As this was the reason that he said that he wanted to postpone taking his exams when the other students did theirs, and why he decided that he would take them in the autumn of that year. He thought that delaying them, would give him a better result in the end!

Now we hadn't been married very long by this time, and I really wanted to help your dad in any way that I could. It wasn't easy, preparing yourself to take your final exams at the University.

And our routine continued, we were now in springtime once again, the weather was so lovely at the time. I know that I was happy, nobody, not even me, could have any doubts that we were anything but happy together!

We continued with our usual routine, I was working and your dad was studying, and then the spring was over and summer had arrived. I thought that everything was good at the time. We had spent time at Easter with your dad's sister and her husband, and some other family members. We also had some outings ourselves, and we also got on with the things that needed to be done, just in the way that you usually do in your life.

Each day I would prepare myself for work, I couldn't expect that anything could possibly be wrong in our lives. I always had the 'Hollywood' idea, that when you fall in love that it will be forever. I can still hear Nat King Cole singing his famous song! We had only been married a short time by then, and no-one could doubt, not even me, that we were anything but happy together, my husband loved me "and only me"!

Here I am singing again! "When I fall in love, it will be forever, or I'll never fall in love"!

Anyway you can tell from my song, that I wasn't expecting what happened next!

One day I was late in leaving for my work, just by coincidence your father left home before me that day. I had no idea where he was going to, the university course was finished by then, and as far as I knew, your dad was spending the maximum time he could in preparation for the autumn exams. I hadn't even thought that I would, or even that I should, check up on my loyal and wonderful husband. I probably did not even ask him where he was going to that day. There was no reason that I should be at all worried, especially about where he went; after all, it was me, and only me that he loved!

Yes, I was always a bit star struck!

So that day when he left home, I did just what the landlady usually did when he left. I went over to the window to wave to him. He didn't look up at the time, he didn't see me looking out of the window, he was probably looking at the landlady's window at the time. But I also became intrigued with where he went that day. He had entered a nearby close where I knew that a very attractive young lady was living at the time. I wasn't worried about this, as I said, I believed that he loved me at the time, but I was rather curious about it all the same!

But we were both in love with each other, so why then would I be worried about what he was doing? Someone once said, that "falling was a fall", (not a success, if you get my meaning), but to star struck me, he had fallen in love with me, and I was the only one he could possibly love. But as I said, I was curious at the time, but not concerned, as until then, he had not given me any cause to be concerned about our relationship.

But you know how our minds keep on ticking over, and as the day went on, I began wondering if this could be the reason that the landlady had been watching him. And of course this made me even more curious about where he could have gone!

I have no idea how long he was there, I did not watch to see him come out of there, in fact I went to work as usual that day. I really thought that he probably had a good reason to go there that day as I had no reason to mistrust him at that time!

As I said, by the time this happened, it was during the summer, and we had not been married one year by then. I hadn't even had any thoughts that my husband might be interested in anyone else, as he loved only me, doesn't that sound so sad? What a fool I was at that time of my life, still am a bit you know!

And as the song goes, "young and foolish", why was I meant to be young and foolish?

But "I don't wish to be young and foolish again"!

As you can tell from what happened next, I had and sometimes still do, have a lot to learn. And so without expecting a bad reaction from your dad, when he returned home later on that day, I made the mistake of asking him about his day and where he had gone to. And during the course of the conversation, I asked him why he had gone into the close (house) where the young lady in question lived.

Much to my shock and horror and with no explanation, my lovely husband grabbed me and started attacking me. He kicked me in the mouth breaking my front tooth, and he punched me in the face, and on my body. I was very badly bruised after this onslaught, and although I did not realise it at the time, this was to be only the first of many beatings that I would have at his hand.

I think I realised then that day, that this was probably the reason that the landlady had been watching him, she was probably just as curious as I was, and of course she was an elderly lady and she understood much more about people than I did at the time.

I can't remember exactly what happened afterwards, all I know was that somehow we seemed to recover from this violent outburst of his. The funny thing is, that after it happened, I was the one who had to apologise to your father. He was not sorry for what he had done to me, because I was the one in the wrong. I shouldn't question him about anything that he was doing, or even ask him the reason why he went there that day!

All I can say is that I think our future lives as a couple, tell me the reason why!

I learned that evening that I must not question your dad about anything, he was always going to be the one in the right, and I must take the blame if ever anything went wrong between us!

You may ask me why I stayed with him, we hadn't been married long, and I think that I must have loved him at the time!

I wonder just how many other women who are mistreated say this!

So after this happened to us, I picked myself up, and I carried on as if nothing had gone wrong between us. I was too immature to know how to deal with something like this, and so I carried on going out to work each day as if nothing had happened.

I should possibly have spoken to my family about it, I may be wrong, but once I had left home, it was almost as if my family did not really have any interest in what happened in my life. They probably thought that once I was married, I would be okay!

I still don't know why he had gone there that day, nor do I know if he continued going there that summer, knowing him now, I expect that he did!

I realised that day that I had married a 'bully', he was going to do just what he wanted, no matter what I said or thought.

So we carried on with our lives, and in the autumn of that year your father took his degree exams, he did pass them, but he didn't get the honours that he said that he had studied all of the summer for, but he accepted this and he started to look for his first job.

Now after your father heard that he had passed his final exams, all of the immediate family members were organised, and they were asked to attend all of the pomp and circumstance of the graduation ceremony. This was a really lovely ceremony. I don't know if you have been to Glasgow University, but it is a really beautiful building or should I say buildings, and well worth a visit. I think that I have a photograph of the event, and if you want to see it, I can show you this.

We all enjoyed this day and I am sure that your grandparents must have been really very proud of their son that day!

What an achievement for any young person!

While your dad was still there at the university, he had some interviews with various employers, and because he had his degree, he was one of the young people who was sought after by several large companies. At the time he accepted a position to go to work for a Company called EMI who were based in Feltham in Middlesex.

I did not realise when I married your father that his work may take us away from my home and my family in Scotland, I had not even considered what would happen to us after he had finished at the university, I think that I must be a 'now' person! But yes, we had to go all the way to England for your father's work. So when we heard this, we had to start making plans for the first of very many moves that we were to make in the future.

So from living our lives in Scotland, your father went to his first job, working for EMI in Feltham, in Middlesex.

My grandmother

Chapter 4
Beginning Our Journey

You know what people say, that life is never dull when you are having fun!

Well as it happened, just as soon as graduation was over, our landlady came to the realisation that we would be leaving our accommodation. She became worried that she may miss the next intake of pupils to the university in the autumn; and as a result of this she asked us to leave our lodgings. And this happened to us, just before it was time for us to organise ourselves for yet another massive change in our lives, as by this time we knew that we were going to leave Scotland and head for a new life in England.

So we had to make our first move, and this was into my family home in Grafton Square, Glasgow. So it was then that we temporarily moved to live with my mother and my sisters. It was from this house that we had to organise ourselves, and get ourselves ready for our journey into the big unknown in England. As I said before, I had not considered that I would leave Scotland when I married your father, although I think that your dad was aware that this was very likely to happen to us.

But during this preparation time I was able to work out my notice with my employer, and when at last we were ready to leave there, we went and we visited all of our friends and our families, and we said our good-byes to everyone!

It was very soon after this that we boarded our trusted motorbike, and we headed out of Glasgow travelling south towards London. Neither of us knew what lay ahead for us in the future, but at least we knew that we had each other to share whatever came up from then on. This time of our lives was really exciting for us, as it was our first big adventure together. We only had a few clothes that were packed in bags, for the start of our new life in England. But I can remember that we were both feeling really happy at the time. How exciting this was for any young couple, we were on our way to a new life in England.

We travelled from Glasgow, going through southern Scotland and onwards on our way, as we were heading south for a short stay in Kettering. We were going into what was for us a completely unknown territory, and also into a completely new country that neither of us knew anything about. We were heading that day for this big adventure and an exciting new life in England. We were enjoying ourselves at this time, as we were both really quite excited about what might lay ahead of us in the future. It was really a lot of fun for both of us, and also very different to anything that we were used to, or had even envisaged. Although it was a good time for us, we found the journey a little bit painful, as we were sitting on our motorbike for that whole day.

We were quite fortunate that your father had relatives living in Kettering, and they were very kind to us, and they put us up for a short time in their nice bungalow.

And as we had expected, your dad's motorbike went very well, and it didn't seem very long to us before we made it to Kettering. We had really enjoyed ourselves, but we were both really pleased when at last we had reached our destination. Your father's aunt and uncle made us feel very welcome in their nice home, and they gave us some comfortable accommodation to live in during the time that we stayed there with them. They knew that we would be moving on again soon, as they knew that your dad had a job to go to.

And it was from their house that we planned our daily trips into the London area, as this was where we started to look for suitable accommodation to move to. We had decided at the time that we wanted to have some accommodation, and be as settled as possible before your father started his new job with EMI in Feltham.

During the time that we stayed in Kettering with your dad's aunt and uncle, we had the opportunity each weekend to visit with some of his other relatives. I don't remember now who they were, but I think that it may have been your dad's cousin, and they had a smallholding somewhere in that area. And it was nice for us to get to know them while we were staying in the area.

Did you know that you may still have relatives in the Kettering area? Another thing I nearly forgot to mention is that you all have a cousin, he is the son of your aunt and uncle who lived in Scotland. The last address that I had for him was where he lived with his father, at 'The Manse', in a place called Gilmerton, which is on the outskirts of Edinburgh. I'm not sure when he was born, but I think that he was born after Ann, and possibly before the birth of Grace, but I could be wrong about the dates.

I don't think at that time that either your dad or I realised just how far it was to travel between London and Feltham. But in fact living in London would have been a big mistake for us, as the distance would have been too much for your dad to travel to work each day.

But getting back to the story, we started our home search in the centre of London, although I do not remember the area that we were searching in. We did find a room to rent, it was in a large house in central London and it was in an extremely dirty house. Fortunately for us we didn't have to stay there long, it was really a bad place for us to be at that time, and we didn't feel at all comfortable living there.

But we soon received some good news from the company who were going to employ your dad, they had found us a flat in the centre of Hounslow in Middlesex. And this flat was only a few miles from Feltham, where your father was going to work. And this apartment was a great start for us and our new lives in England.

We moved into this, it was very adequately furnished and it was really perfect for us. The flat was in the upstairs part of a family house, and the family who owned it all lived in the downstairs part of the house. We had a very large lounge, a bedroom, a bathroom, and a very warm kitchen to live in during the time that we were there. We soon settled into the flat, as it was a very easy journey for your dad when he travelled to work, and I also managed to get some accounts work in a local company who were based nearby. This was really a good start for us, as it meant that we became a bit more financially secure as a couple.

We started to make friends with the people that I was meeting at my place of work, and also with people that your dad was meeting where he was working. During all of the time that we lived there, we attended a local Baptist church. One of the things that I got the opportunity to do while we were there was to lead a small group of girls who after a time were able to do the bulk of the singing for the special music in the church. Doing this was a most enjoyable thing for me to do. I loved to hear the young girls singing for the church special music.

While we were living there in Hounslow, we always seemed to have a few problems. Your father always seemed to be a little bit more interested in very young girls than seemed to be healthy for our marriage. And at the time, the girls who were in my singing group were all very young. Now this did come up in conversation from time to time, as I was always concerned about this. I knew your dad quite well by now, and I also knew that I was not allowed to question him about any of his friendships. This was always a no go area for us, as your father could turn very angry and even violent at any moment in time, and especially if I questioned him about any of his actions. And even although I was worried about things that were happening, I tried to brush off any incidents by not taking them too seriously. After all it was me who he loved, wasn't it?

By this time in our lives, I did know your dad and how he would react quite well. I can even remember when we were living in Scotland that we had some problems (and I think that this was even before we were married). If I would not give in to him in anything that he wanted, he would lie in bed and he would tell me that he was going to die, and this was to try to force me to do what he wanted. So I became used to his strange behaviour, and I did my best not to question him about anything if at all possible, just in case he did not like it!

We also got friendly with some people who your father worked with, I can remember that at one time we started to fence while we lived there, but for some reason this all came to a quick and sudden end.

Whatever we did always had to be the things that your dad wanted to do!

One of the couples who we would spend quite a lot of time with, were your dad's closest friend at work and his wife. During the time of the friendship we would go over to their home, or they would come to ours. And it was during one of these visits to their home, that I was asked if I would do a wife swap with them. I have no idea who among us was interested in doing this, I knew that I did not want to, and I did not discuss it with anyone. Now this may seem strange to you, but at this particular time it was known that many couples engaged in this kind of behaviour.

And it was also during this time, that we would travel quite a lot backwards and forwards to see our families in Scotland. We lived near to Hounslow airport, and we would travel from Hounslow to either Glasgow or Edinburgh airport quite regularly.

We loved to go back home, as we loved being with the people who were our friends and our families. On one of our visits to Scotland, we picked up our first car that your grandfather had bought for us. He had been working on it for some time and making it roadworthy for us. And he did this to make it more affordable for us, and also to make it possible for us to travel up there to Scotland more often. It was always very expensive to travel by air, and having the car would mean that we could go more often to visit with our relatives. I recently showed you a photograph of that car, it was a Ford Consul and it was painted red and black.

As I said before, your grandfather on your dad's side was always so kind to us, he really did love his son very much. He must have hoped that by giving us this car that we would be able to go back to Scotland to see them a bit more often. This was the first car that we owned, and your granddad had painted the bottom half of the car red. So at this time in our lives we had a black and red Ford Consul car to travel about in. We loved our new car, and we were able to travel backwards and forwards regularly in it.

And it was also around this time, that we started our journeys each weekend into the centre of London, as we wanted to visit the many sights that they had in London. We really enjoyed ourselves on these visits. I can remember that we went to Hyde Park corner, and we listened to people giving speeches at Speaker's Corner. We would walk in the park, and we would walk along Oxford Street and go into Selfridges. We also visited many of the other large shops that were there in the heart of London. On another visit we went to Harrods store, Madame Tussauds, and the Planetarium. Usually after eating out in a nice restaurant, we would spend our time taking in a show or a cinema. I can remember that on one occasion when we went there, we heard the Red Army sing in concert in one of the large theatres in London. We also went on at least one occasion to the biggest bookshop in the country.

The world was our oyster, or at least London was for us at that time!

And of course everything was fine in our marriage, just so long as I did whatever it was your father wanted. We did have some disagreements during these early days. I think that our main problem was because of your father's weird interest in young girls in particular. Everywhere we made friends, he would pick out someone (usually younger than us) who was special to him, and of course I was always in the wrong if I objected to this. If I asked him about it, I was told that I was jealous, and that there was nothing for me to be concerned about.

I think that by now, that this was a time bomb waiting to happen!

Now around this time we heard of the well-known film called Summer Holiday, the one that both Cliff Richard and the Young Ones filmed. How exciting was that! We both saw this film several times, and we loved the film and everything that went along with it. Each time that we saw it, we were convinced that this was what we wanted to do in the future. And of course what did we do next, yes you guessed, it was then that we took our first trip to a travel agent, and we arranged to go on our very first continental holiday in the sun the following year.

So the time of the holiday soon came around, I nearly missed a cue for a song....

'We're all going on a summer holiday, no more working for a week or two,

Fun and laughter on a summer holiday, doing all the things you want to do, for me and you

We're going where the sun shines brightly, we're going where the sea is blue

We've seen it in the movies, let's see if it's true.'

The first year that we went abroad on holiday we flew to a place called Liguria this is a lovely place on the Mediterranean side of Italy. Because we loved Italy so much, we decided to go the following year to a place on the Adriatic, which is the western side of Italy. We really enjoyed these times that we had together, and we stayed in hotel type accommodation during these holidays. While we were there, we spent most of our time soaking up the lovely sunshine during the day. In the evenings we would find a place where we could spend the evening dancing, and listening to music. Afterwards we would walk in the cool of the night, before we headed off to bed.

Yes, we loved the times that we spent in Italy, and it was while we were on this holiday, that we took a coach trip to Rome to see the Colosseum, the Trevi fountain and the other amazing sights that there are there.

Sunny summer holidays, doesn't it all sound so lovely!

So after our holidays were over, we both got down to the day to day things that happen in everyone's life, and this included some hard work from both of us. It also included a few journeys home to see our families in Scotland.

But we were having such a great time on these holidays, we had loved the beautiful sunshine and the relaxed atmosphere that there was abroad, the following year we decided that we would take our car with us, as we thought that we could have an extended family holiday on the continent. We purchased two large orange boxes, we painted them both black to match the car, and when the time for the holiday came, we put them on to the car roof rack full of pots and pans and many tins of food. We bought ourselves a walk-in tent, as we wanted to have as nice an accommodation as possible while we were away, and with everything packed, we headed for the ferry, as this time we planned to stay away for a whole month.

On this trip we travelled through Brussels, down into France, Switzerland and Austria and on until we reached the northern part of Italy. We spent some time there in the Italian mountains, only leaving when the weather broke, and we then quickly packed our belongings and headed for our favourite spot near Nice, on the Mediterranean side of Italy.

As I said, in between all of these enjoyable times that we were having, we continued with our work and our lives. I think that it was at this time that your dad decided to teach me to drive, and so we spent quite a long time on this, as I was the world's worst driver to start with, as I even had to learn to steer the car. I did find it all very difficult, but I am so glad now that I continued with this, as I have been able to drive ever since your dad taught me.

Everything seemed fine for us at that time of our lives, and we were really enjoying the very nice place that we were living in.

So after the first camping holiday that we went on, we were really smitten with continental holidays, and we started to plan to do this again the following year. So the following year we travelled again by car, and we went down through France, Switzerland, and Austria, and then down into Italy. I think that by this time, Italy was our favourite place to visit. On this camping holiday we camped again around Liguria as this was our favourite spot on the Mediterranean. While we were there, we once again soaked up the warm sunny days. We also did a lot of walking at the time. In the evenings we would walk to the nearest dance venue. We really did have some lovely times while we were there, weren't we both so lucky at this time of our life!

After our holiday was over, we came back home again to Hounslow. Just like they did in the film, we had enjoyed a lovely time again in Italy, and we continued to get on with our lives there in Hounslow. And it was only when I worked out the holidays that we had on the continent, that I realised that we had stayed in the same accommodation in Hounslow for about five years, and this was almost all of the time that we had been married by this time.

But no sooner were we back from our holiday than we were once again planning our next trip away. We continued with our work and looking after our home; life seemed fairly good to me at this time, as we were continuing to have some really good times as young people do. We loved where we lived in Hounslow, and also the time that we spent travelling around the various parts of London. It sounds here as if life was one big holiday for us, but we did work hard to earn the money to do these things. We didn't have any children, and we did not have the responsibility of a mortgage hanging around our heads at this time of our lives.

Now it was during the time that we stayed in Hounslow, that my friends (I told you before about the lady and her daughter who played the accordion), they would come down from Scotland to Hounslow on a visit to see us. It was during one of their visits to see us, and after we had told them about our trips to the continent, that they said that they would like to accompany us on our next continental holiday. So with both of them as excited as we were about this as an idea, we all started preparing for a holiday together the following summer.

And so the time went by very quickly, and it wasn't long before our friends flew down once again from Glasgow to meet with us at Hounslow airport. At the time we were all looking forward to sharing our holiday in the sun together. So the following day after they had rested from their journey from Scotland, we all set off to find the sea, and of course the wonderful sunshine that they have in Europe. We spent our time while we were over there camping and touring around the continent, and we showed our friends the many sights that we knew about as we travelled down through Europe. We did have some laughs together, especially at some of the toilet facilities that we found in France, and sadly the time seemed to go all too quickly, as before long it was time for the return trip home again.

Anyway once we were back home again, we saw our friends off at the airport, and as usual we got on with our work, and with our lives, as we were well settled there in Hounslow by this time. I remember that we did have an incident, I can't even remember what caused it, but I do know that I went into London and I stayed there in a

96

women's hostel at one point, only to be asked to come back home later by your father.

As I said though, we were continuing to get on with the many things in our lives, and with our various jobs that we had to do. But during all of this time, we kept thinking and talking about the wonderful holidays that we had on the continent, they had really drawn us in, and we really loved going there. And so it was then that we decided that we would have another continental holiday the following year. Now as the time got nearer, the conversations started once again with the guests who had accompanied us the previous year. I was told that the mum of the family could not come with us, and that only the young girl was going to accompany us on the holiday this time.

Anyway with sunshine and fun again in our minds, we waited for the holiday time to arrive, and when the time came, we went to the airport to pick up the young girl, as she was going to accompany us on this year's holiday.

Our final destination was Italy, we both loved it there, and we also loved touring and staying in the various camp sites, just as we usually did. So we set off once again, we knew that we had a month of enjoyment ahead of us, and we planned to both camp and tour during the time that we were away. The young girl who was with us was my friend's youngest daughter. I had known her since she was four years old, her mum had introduced me to my Glasgow singing teacher when I was younger, and I knew the family quite well by this time. I had known this girl ever since I heard her play the accordion, when we both performed in concerts in Glasgow when I had lived there.

I loved having the girl on holiday with us, both she and her mum were always very special to me, as they were like family to me. Some of my happiest memories were the ones that I had shared with them in the past. But it was strange that during the time of the holiday, I noticed that your dad was being more than friendly towards her. Now he said that I was 'jealous', now I hated being called this, it is quite a cop out! The girl was very young at this time, and I should not mind the attention that he was giving her. But you know what; I was told as usual that I was wrong for noticing anything as nothing could be wrong.

So at the time, I did as I usually did in these sort of circumstances, I put any thoughts or even resentments that were building in me, completely out of my head. After all I would be in a lot of trouble with your dad, especially if I did anything to upset him. I knew that he always reacted badly if I said anything that he did not like.

So once again, we were all enjoying the lovely time that we were having, with so many nice places to see, nobody could fail to enjoy all of the good times that we were all having together.

So as they all do, our holiday was gradually coming to an end, yet another month had flown by and sadly we had to start packing up our belongings once again. We knew that the following day we were going to start on the return journey back home.

Now on any journey that we took during this period of time, your father and I would share the driving equally, as this seemed to make any journey that we took go much quicker for us. And it also made it easier to cover some of the distances that we would often travel together. And so the morning of the day that we were leaving on our way home was no exception to this.

We each had our time at the wheel of the car scheduled out, and your father was the first to take a turn at the wheel. We had a long way to drive that day, as we had to reach Dover in the early hours of the following morning. Now we must have travelled a long way, I know that I was having my turn driving, and it was getting darker and darker and I felt that I could not continue to drive any more at the time. Your father said that I should stop the car and he would take over the driving. And at that same time he suggested that I lie in the back of the car and have a sleep. So without thinking any more about it, I did what he said as by this time I was feeling very tired, I opened the back door of the car and lay down, and I must have fallen asleep.

While I was doing this your father took another turn at the wheel and he started to drive once again. He had to continue driving because we were on a limited time schedule, as we had to get to the sea port by early the next morning.

Now some time later when I woke up, I was very surprised that the car was stationary. But I was even more surprised when I looked over from the back seat, and I saw your father with his arms around the girl while they were sitting there on the front seat of the car. Now I am not saying here that anything bad happened at that time, as I had just woken from being asleep at the time; I will never know the answer to this; as I was too afraid to even broach the subject with your dad after this. I knew that it would perhaps cause some kind of scene if I asked him, and I didn't want that to happen.

After this we took the young girl back to her home in Scotland, and no-one said anything at all about this to me. We only went to their home once after that, it was during a trip that we took to Scotland for the Christmas holidays. We did go on a visit to see them at the time, and it seemed to me that we had rather a cold reception from them; and that was the last time I saw any of them.

What I would like to add here, if nothing happened, and it probably didn't, your dad didn't mind putting our marriage at risk during the time that we were together. But I guess that many young men take risks with their relationship and think nothing of it.

All I knew was that we both loved these times that we shared abroad, and I can honestly say that we did seem to have some measure of happiness in our friendship!

But I think that by now alarm bells should have been ringing in my head! You can see by now, that there were some very serious flaws in our relationship!

With my first bike in Glasgow

Chapter 5
A Fresh Start in Bolton

Now it was very soon after our last continental holiday together, that your father started to get itchy feet. It turned out that his best friend at work came in one day, and he announced to them all that he was leaving his job. And this was soon after another member of staff who they had both worked with had also left the company. It seemed that none of them were happy continuing to work on the guided missile program that they had been employed to do.

Now your father's best friend managed to get himself a teaching job, it was in one of the colleges back home in Ireland and in the area that they had come from. And at the time that this happened, the idea of teaching really appealed to your father. He decided there and then that he would also try to find a teaching post, and this would hopefully be in Britain, and somewhere that they could use the kind of skills that he had to offer.

As a result of this he started his job search by applying to the various colleges in England. Just by coincidence they were looking for someone to work on the teaching staff at the Blackburn Technical College in Lancashire at the time. They were looking for someone who could teach the students, and your father had the kind of experience and the qualifications that they required. So he applied for the position, and after having an interview with them they offered him the job that they were advertising.

Your father changing his job at this time would mean a big change for us as a couple. It would mean that we would have to leave our base, the home that we had lived in for about the last five years in Hounslow. We had been happy there for most of the time, and we had gradually become very settled there. But now we had to get used to another big change, and so we travelled up to the Blackburn area, and we started to look around for a suitable place for us to live. During our search we managed to find a small furnished house in a small town called Darwen, this house was fairly near to Blackburn where your father was going to be working, and at the time we thought that this would be a suitable place for us to live.

So now that we knew where we were going to be based, all we had to do was to go back to our respective employers, and hand them in our leaving notice. Another thing that we knew we had to do at this time was to hand in our notice to the nice family whose house we had been living in for the last five years; ever since we arrived in England.

So after we had done all of the things that we had to do in Hounslow, we then did the packing of all of our clothes, and our other personal belongings. And when we were finally ready for take-off, we said our goodbyes to the friends that we had made, and also to the various other people that we knew within the local area. When we thought that we had taken care of everything, we loaded up the car, and we were then on our way and heading for a new home in Lancashire.

We soon made friends when we arrived there in Darwen, as you seem to make friends much more easily when you are young, or perhaps it is just because you go out more? Our new home was quite an old house, and at the time that we rented it, it badly needed some TLC; but nothing that we could not do between ourselves for us to be happy with it. After a massive clean-up I soon had it shipshape, and we were then comfortable in our new home. It was quite a change from what we were used to, it was bigger than where we had lived before, but even at that we soon settled down there.

I think that if I remember rightly, that it was here while we were in this area that your dad took over the responsibility of the running of a youth club, the club was connected to a church that we had started to attend at this time. So as you can see, we really started to get ourselves involved in the local community in that area.

Unfortunately, because we were in a recession at the time, I couldn't find any accounts work to do in the local area. Instead of doing accounts for a living, I did some door to door canvassing as I hoped that I would earn some money by doing this. Later on I tried selling vacuum cleaners by going door to door and demonstrating them.

It was now well into the autumn and it had started to get really cold in Darwen. I can remember that it was so very cold during that winter; and because we lived at the top of a hill; we had to put snow tyres on our Consul car to get us to the top of the hill each day. When we were working my colleagues and I would walk about the streets, we were knocking on the doors of houses, asking them if we could demonstrate the lovely machines that we were selling. Every so often, we were so cold that we had to stop what we were doing and find a café or somewhere else where we could sit down and have a warm. It seemed unbearable to us walking about in such bad weather. It seemed as if the winter was especially bad that year. I do not know it, but perhaps it is always as cold as it was there at that time of year.

So we found ourselves living there in this cold and very damp area, and your father didn't like it at all. I was also finding the cold too much to take, as I was out there trailing the streets selling vacuum cleaners to the householders in the area. But we both continued on with our respective jobs as we had already made the decision to move away again, and we had to accept the conditions that we were in at that time.

So we continued to live there in Darwen, as we knew by now that we would move again the following year. Your father had already decided that he wanted to move down to the south of England to live once again.

So because the weather conditions were so bad that winter, we began to spend a lot of our leisure time at home. And during this time we were also thinking about what we would like to do for the future. It wasn't really a very hard decision for either of us, as we both decided that we would like to go back to live somewhere in the southern part of England. Firstly, because we had both enjoyed living there so much, and also because we had found that it was warmer there in the winter. So with this decision made, your father just had to see out the contract that he had agreed to do at the college. We knew that this contract would finish at the end of the college year, and in the meantime, your dad was going to try his best to find another college to teach in a bit further south.

Now, it was during this time when we were spending a lot of our time at home, that your father was tuning in to the radio quite a lot. And that was when he heard a broadcast coming over from Radio Caroline, the pirate radio ship. Your dad got very fascinated and interested in the things that they were saying on this broadcast. This was when he was listening to a broadcast that was called 'The World Tomorrow'. And it wasn't long after this that we began listening regularly to this broadcast coming over from radio Caroline.

We did this for quite a period of time, we were both still attending a Baptist church in the Darwen area where we lived, and we were both working and planning our future together. But we were more than a little intrigued by this message coming from Radio Caroline called 'The World Tomorrow', as it seemed that they were able to answer a lot of questions that had remained un-answered in our minds for a long time.

After talking about it, we began wondering if there might be either a church, or some people who met together, and who were connected to the broadcast.

So your father decided at the time, that he would try to find out some more information about what we were hearing. And at the time he replied to an address that they were giving out at the end of the broadcast. I know that it was shortly after this that we started receiving a course called 'The Ambassador College Correspondence Course'; and this was only one of the booklets that they

106

were offering free of charge at the time. As we found out later, all of the literature that they sent out was given free of charge to whoever asked for it.

And so this was what we started to do with our time, we did the correspondence course, and at the same time we were still listening avidly to the broadcast that was coming over the radio. We were soaking up any information that we could from these broadcasts.

As I said this broadcast coming over the air from Radio Caroline was giving us the answer to many of the questions that we had at the time, both about our future, and also the future of the world. And because of this, we decided that we would pursue this as fully as we could.

It was also during this time that your father started applying for different teaching positions in the southern part of England, and we were really happy when we heard that one of these had become available at the Wimbledon Technical College. So your dad got himself organised, and he took a trip down there to Wimbledon, and he had an interview with the college authorities. He was obviously very blessed over his work, as he managed to secure a position with the college that very day.

After we found out where we were going, we obviously had to start thinking of where we were going to live in the Wimbledon area. It was while we were talking it over that your dad decided that it was now time for us to buy our first home together. We realised then that it would be a good idea if we could manage to find a house somewhere near to the college, to be as close as possible to where your dad was going to work.

So the next thing for your dad to do was to give in his notice to the relevant people at the college in Blackburn.

And it was after this that we were able to start our serious house search. We started looking in the area around where Wimbledon Technical College was based, all this took place years before you could look up houses for sale on the internet. It meant that we had to wait for the post, and also take some trips down there and spend our time searching out the various properties that were available and on the market at that time.

All during this time of our lives though, we were still continuing with our work, and we were also spending any spare time that we had doing the correspondence course that we had sent off for. We were so excited about what we were reading, that we requested further booklets from them. We wanted to understand as fully as possible about what we were hearing. All of these things were having a big impact on our lives, and we were very excited and anxious to have as much information as we could about what they were saying.

For some time in the past we had called ourselves "Christian". We had together attended Baptist churches wherever we went. We had also run a small youth group in one of the churches in our area. As you can imagine, this broadcast that we were hearing was giving us some serious thoughts about the things that we believed in. And consequently after doing a lot of homework on this, we asked if we could have a home visit from someone who was in this organisation, and it was from this time onwards that we had a weekly visit to our home.

So this became a regular thing for us, because after requesting it, we began to have a weekly visit from a gentleman from this organisation. We were really very happy about this, as we were really keen to know even more about the things that we were hearing on the radio broadcast. It turned out that our visitor was a minister from this church, but one of the striking things that I noticed was that he didn't wear a dog collar on any of his visits, and this made the atmosphere much more relaxing for all of us.

I do not remember the length of time that we lived in that house in Darwen in Lancashire. I do know that your dad only worked at the college in Blackburn for the one college year, and so I expect that it was less than a year. I do know that we had not been there very long when we had started planning to move again. Your dad was really certain at the time that he did not want to continue living there in the cold north of England.

But he decided that he was happy that he had chosen to go into teaching, and he was already looking forward to his new position at the Wimbledon Technical College.

Now I can still remember the time that we spent house hunting around the Wimbledon area. It was the summer time, and the weather was beautiful, and your father and I started our house search in the area near to Wimbledon. We knew by then that we were going to buy our first home together, and so consequently, we started visiting estate agents in the area. All we knew was that we were looking for somewhere suitable for us as this was our first house purchase.

We started our property search by looking at houses around the Worcester Park area, we saw some lovely properties at the time, and we really liked the idea of living in that area. After looking at several lovely properties, we finally decided to buy a lovely detached bungalow that was in Worcester Park in Surrey. This was our first choice after seeing some really beautiful properties, and it was the first and the only home that we ever bought together.

The bungalow was very spacious, it was certainly big enough for the two of us, and it had a nice and simple front garden. The garden at the back of the house was a very large plot; it had a lawn, borders and a large area that was a plot for growing vegetables. We both loved it, and we especially loved the lovely big garden that the house had.

So after choosing our bungalow, we travelled up north again to Darwen. When we arrived there we did all of the organising and planning that had to be done there. We also had to pack our clothes and our personal belongings ready for the move, and after completing everything and we were ready to leave, we said our goodbyes to the people who were our friends by this time.

Very soon after this we received the good news that our house purchase had been completed, and we were told that we could move into our new home. So here we were once more on the move, only this time we were heading for Surrey and our first new home together.

With my sisters in Glasgow

Chapter 6
Living in Surrey

As you can imagine, this was very exciting for us. We moved into the bungalow, and because we didn't have any furniture or furnishings (as we had always rented property), we found it really exciting to organise the things that we needed for our new home. I can still remember being thrilled by the lovely Moffat cooker that we bought, such a lovely bit of equipment, it even had its very own spit for roasting. We decorated the whole of the bungalow from top to bottom, and then we had our new carpets fitted. And all this work was done before the arrival of our furniture. How exciting was this for us! Neither of us had done anything like this before.

And it wasn't long after we moved in there that your father started his next new job. He soon settled into his new position at Wimbledon Technical College, and he seemed at the time to be very happy working there, and also very happy that we had moved south again. It was also really lucky for us, as I managed to get myself a position working in Bentalls department store doing statistics.

It was such a great privilege for me to work there, I loved being in their large and very beautiful store. The

Bentalls department store wasn't very far for me to travel from our home in Worcester Park, and it brought back to me very many memories of the time that I had worked in Glasgow for Muirhead's, the place that I had worked for years and almost up until a short time before your dad and I were married.

Life seemed really good at this time, it certainly was for me. Things were really looking up for us, we had good jobs, nice things, a lovely home to live in, and it was such a lovely summer that year, and when we had any spare time, we spent it working in our lovely garden.

I loved your dad, we did sometimes have some problems, but this was only occasionally, and it was always over the same thing. He didn't like it if I objected at times over the very obvious attention that he gave the very young girls that we met. But everything seemed okay with us, just so long as I did not ask him any questions at all about this. Any sign of resistance from me over anything that your dad did or wanted to do, would always lead us to an unpleasant scene, and he could end up becoming violent. It was strange, I wasn't stopping him doing the things that he wanted to do, but I was forced to go along and agree with whatever it was that he wanted to do.

But at the same time, it was lovely living there at that time in Worcester Park, it was such a nice spot to live in, and to me we both seemed to be happy while we lived there. We also travelled up to Scotland from time to time to see our relatives, and we were able to go into London once again, just as we had done when we lived in the Hounslow area.

So here we were once again going into the centre of London each weekend, we would go to see the various shows that were showing at the time. We loved going to the shows and the movies that were on at the time, and we always spent part of our time doing our shopping and eating out. It wasn't that we were well off, but we didn't have any children, because at that time your dad said that he did not want children. We were both in good jobs and we were earning enough money each month to live quite comfortably.

And so this became the norm for us, we were both going out to work during each week, and at the weekend we would travel into the centre of London on a Saturday, we had the money that we had earned, and we enjoyed ourselves. We took in all kinds of shows, pictures, dancing, late night movies and the many of the other things that you could find to do in London. Neither of us had to be worried about money, and we would often go out for meals while we were there.

I can remember though, that we had one incident when we were in London. I wasn't happy to go into one of the clubs that your dad wanted to see, I didn't like the idea of it, but it was probably quite tame compared to what they show you on the television today. But as was usually the case in our relationship, any resistance from me always led to an unpleasant scene, and could also end up with me being hurt or bruised. It was really strange to me, but I was forced to go along with, and do, whatever it was that your dad wanted to do.

So the scene was set, with many beatings and bruisings along the way. We, or should I say that I, carried on in this relationship that was very one-sided.

Your dad was just a bully, and I had to go along with whatever he asked, or whatever he wanted to do all of the time!

Your father was so violent to me that I now have very bad scarring to my right eye. Many years ago when I had it checked out at a hospital, I was told that the only thing that could be done for it, was for me to have an eye transplant, and I really would not like to have this done. This is not obvious when you look at me, but in a recent eye test, the technician showed me the scarring on the computer, and even I was shocked at just how bad it is.

Things always had to be done your father's way, or else! I loved your dad, and it was always much easier for me if I went along with what he wanted, no questions asked!

Now I think that most people who were looking at the both of us would have thought how lucky we were. We had each other, we had good jobs, and we had a lovely home to live in. But none of these people that we knew were aware of the problems that we were having, but the problems were always there in the background.

Although they may be different ones, it is probably like that for most couples!

But gradually things began to change for us, our lives started changing and for the better. Some of these unpleasant episodes became a thing of the past, no, it wasn't that we had won the lottery (well there wasn't one then), but together we embraced this new way of life that we were learning about on the broadcasts. The broadcasts and the visits that we were having were having a big impact on us as people, and your father seemed to become much happier and settled as a person, and these changes were all for the good for us as a couple.

As you can tell from my last statement, we were both still listening to the weekly broadcasts from Radio Caroline, and at the same time, we were learning the things that we were being taught when we were doing the correspondence course. We had also managed to find out that there was a church somewhere in the London area. We were young and enjoying our lives at this time, so all we had to do was to find out if we could attend the church in London, as this would enable us to learn more about the things that we had been hearing.

So after finding out where the people met, and also hearing that these people met on a Saturday, all we had to do was to ask the minister if we could go there. We were so pleased when we were told that we could, as we were really curious to find out as much as we could about these people. We were both used to travelling weekly into the city, and this gave us a real reason to go there, apart from just having a good time when we went there.

So this was when we first started attending this new church, our Saturday in London began to take on a completely different meaning for both of us. It didn't take very long before your father seemed to become embroiled with this new way of life that we had started to learn about. And we began to have some wonderful times when we went along there, as we were meeting and getting to know the various people who went there.

Unknown to us at that time, our lives would change rather a lot from this time onwards. I hadn't at any time met such nice people, and going there on a Saturday was helping us to change and to become better people ourselves, perhaps you know, we were even growing up!

This then, was the best thing that could have happened to us as a couple, we began to make new friends with the lovely people that we were meeting, everything was new to us, and we were very happy with the things that we were learning.

The changes in our lives were all for the good, as far as I was concerned. And we were starting to build up long-term friendships with some of the people who we were meeting there. It seemed as though most of the couples who were there had children, and we seemed to stand out quite a bit, as we had not had any children by this time.

And so we continued to go to the meetings each week, and we continued making friends and enjoying our time there. Now it is at this point in the story, that I want to mention one family in particular that we met there, this family were to feature in our lives, both at this time, and into our future. This is where we met them, there in London in the church that we all attended. And this couple and their children continued to be involved in our lives from both then, and into the years to come.

Now this family became very close friends of ours, you will know who I am talking about, because you all know what happened many years later, but I am not going to call them by their real name, and so I have given them the fictitious name of Davis, as this will make it easier for me when telling you the rest of this story.

This couple that I am referring to then (as I said I am going to call them the Davis family), they were both a bit older than we were, as they already had five children in

117

their family by this time. They had a boy and girl who had already left home by the time that we met them, and they still had one teenage daughter, and an even younger daughter, and an even younger son, and they all lived together with their parents. And they were the family that we got to know, and they became our best friends.

Now as you probably know, your dad is, or certainly was, a bit of a perpetual student, as he seemed to love learning new things all of the time. And it was on these trips that we took to London that we started to regularly meet with the college students from Ambassador College. Meeting them made your dad become even more curious, and more interested in the work that they were doing. Most of these students were in this country from many countries all around the world, and it was always interesting to talk with them and to get to know them. We made friends with some of them, and your father got more and more interested in what was happening in the organisation, and in particular what was happening at the college.

When the students were there on Saturdays, it was usually to help in the speaking assignments, and they would also do any of the special music that they had there, and so for us, it was always a special treat to spend some of our time with them, and to find out more about the college that they were attending.

So for some after this, we would spend as much time as we could with the students while we were there, and I think that your father already had his next plan formulating in his mind at that time. He was finding out about the college, what happened there, about the tuition etc., as he was beginning to think that he would like to go there to study.

We discussed this at home, yes, I was correct, your father was thinking at the time of giving up his job at Wimbledon Technical College, to go to Ambassador College, and become a student once again. So it will not come as a big surprise when I tell you what was going to be the next big event in our lives.

On one occasion that we went there for the afternoon meeting, your father spoke to one of the ministers who had been teaching us that day. Your father had already decided by then that he should ask the question about how he could go about applying to the college as a student.

So with this in his mind, he approached the minister, and your father invited him to come to visit us in our home the next time that he was in the area. The reason was clear to me at least, he wanted to ask the question: could he attend Ambassador College?

So the next time the minister came over to London, he brought his wife and his son with him, and after the services were over, they all came over to our home to visit with us. It was a long way round for them to travel, as they lived in Bricket Wood at the time. Their journey was from Bricket Wood to central London, from central London to Worcester Park in Surrey, and then from our home, back to Bricket Wood.

I did my best to cook some kind of dinner for all of us to enjoy, and they all seemed to enjoy the time that they had with us. During the course of the visit, your dad asked the minister about the possibility of him attending the college in Bricket Wood as a student.

Now you may wonder why he would need to do this, he already had a Bachelor of Science degree from Glasgow University, and he had letters from several other organisations by this time. But here he was, very set on continuing studying for a further degree, as he wanted to learn more about this new way of life that we were hearing about!

We obviously could not have an answer that day, your father would have to be interviewed properly by other college officials at the college, but this did not put your father off from trying, as you know if he wants to do something, he gets very determined, and he was really sure that this was what he wanted to do at that time. I think that the first time that he asked, they said no to him. I think that this must have been during the winter, because by the spring he was once again asking them about it, as he really wanted to start at the college the following autumn. He knew that he would have to give notice at the technical college where he was working, in order to be able to leave at the end of the college year.

But perhaps because he was so certain that this was what he wanted to do, we were asked to go to the college campus for interviews. The college officials had to find out if we would be suitable, and if we would fit in with the student body who were mostly single people.

We had been to the college on a previous occasion, and we were really impressed by what we saw there, and I think that on that visit, your father was even more convinced than ever that this was what he wanted to do for the future.

This was really a very exciting time for us, we were asked to go for interviews, and when we arrived there that day, you know that when you can't believe what is happening to you, you go ahead with your heart in your mouth, and hope that it works out for you. Well it was a bit like that for us that day, we were both holding our breath and hoping that we would get some good news, as by this time, this was what we both wanted to do.

So all we had to do was get over the first hurdle of the two interviews, and then we hoped that the people at the college would like us enough for us to be accepted to go there. Your father was the important one, he was the one who was going to be the student, but they liked to know that I was going to be supportive, as this was going to be a very big change in our lives. It seemed as though they were very impressed by what your dad had achieved at such a young age. And it was at that time that we were given the go ahead to re-locate to the Bricket Wood campus. They knew that we needed time to get ourselves organised and ready for your dad to begin his studies at the college the following autumn!

This then was a massive change for us, and here we were once again on the move. The difference this time was that we would have to sell our lovely bungalow, and go back to live in rented accommodation. So we put our house on to the market, and hoped that we would find a buyer soon to take it off of our hands.

We then needed an empty place to live, our furniture was fairly new and we needed an accommodation where we could take it with us. We were really blessed that the college had a department that dealt with housing, and we were given a flat to live in. The flat was in a place called Marshalswick, which was just outside of St. Albans. This area was only a short drive from the college, and your dad would have to travel from there to the college each day.

So this then was another beginning for us; with an exciting future stretched out before us; and a new life at an amazing place, we were now on our way to Ambassador College!

Our bantam major motorbike

Chapter 7
Our Life at Ambassador College

It wasn't much of a struggle for us to make this move to Ambassador College, from the moment that we made the decision to go there ourselves, and then of course, when we were given the go-ahead from the college, everything seemed to go like clockwork for us. We were also really pleased when we heard the news that the housing department at the college had managed to find us a small unfurnished flat for us to live in. The flat that we were to rent was in a place called Marshalswick, which is very near to St. Albans. After receiving this good news, we began to really look forward to the time when we could get ourselves re-settled, and get ourselves ready for your dad's first semester at the college. The flat in Marshalswick was only a short commute to the college campus in Bricket Wood, the place where your dad would be beginning his studies.

So we went back home, and we spent the necessary time getting ourselves organised for this new move. I was still working at Bentalls in Kingston at the time, and I gave my notice in to them. At the same time, your father had to give his notice to his superiors at the Wimbledon

Technical College, as he was now leaving there at the end of the college year. We put our house on to the market, and we got a buyer for this very quickly. Everything seemed to be working out well for us, so we packed up our home and we arranged for the removal of our furniture to Marshalswick. From that moment, we were on our way to a very different kind of future.

Ambassador College was a co-ed college, and most of the students who attended there had travelled there to study from various countries all around the world. The students all lived in dormitories on the college campus, but because we were a married couple, we were going to be living off of the campus. I remember thinking that the two bedroomed flat that we had been given to live in was very adequate for us, and we soon settled down into our new routine when we arrived there.

I would like to add here that the changes that we were making to our lives were the best thing that we or anyone could experience. Ambassador College was certainly a unique place to be!

I know that as the future events unfold, that it was very tragic for us as a family. But this was not in any way the fault of the college, or the systems that were in place there. It was the fault of the time bomb that I have already said was waiting to happen in our lives. As I said previously, we had some very serious flaws in our marriage and in our relationship!

After your dad had started his new course, and for a long period of time after this, he seemed to be embroiled with the new way of life that we were learning about. I have to continue telling you about our life at the college, as it was here where our lives changed, and it was here where I lost you all!

Life at Ambassador College was the most wonderful experience that anyone could have. After we got settled into our new home, we began by attending the commencement exercises at the college. It started with an amazing ball which was attended by all of the students and the faculty. And of course we were now a part of the student body, and we were of course expected to attend this. The young men looked really smart and dashing in their evening attire, and the ladies were stunning in their long evening dresses. They all danced around the lovely floor, they talked with each other, ate nice food, and there were a lot of happy reunions for the students who had been there during the previous years.

What a start to a very exciting future for all of us, I thought!

We really enjoyed ourselves that evening, and after the ball was over (I think that this is a queue for another song), we went home even more excited about the future that lay ahead of us. When we got home that evening, we were feeling tired with all of the dancing that we had done that night, but we had both felt that we had a really lovely time that evening. The following day your father headed for the campus, as he had to spend some time meeting the students who were going to be in his class that year. Obviously I was not there with him, as I was home trying to organise our flat, but I know that your dad was happy to be going there to the college, as he was now ready to start his first year as a freshman.

At Ambassador College all of the students did the basic work of cleaning and organising at the campus, as they all contributed to the smooth running of the college. They each had their various jobs to do, as this was how they financed their way, and it meant that they were able to continue with their studies each year. At the time that we arrived there, the college couldn't offer your dad any work on the campus, but fortunately because your dad had taught at a college before, he managed to find himself some work, and he began teaching part-time at the Watford Technical College a couple of evenings each week. Later on the college gave him some janitorial work on the campus, and all of this was to help support us while we were there. Your dad seemed very happy to do this, as we also had to finance our way there!

The things that they did there at the college were so good, and they seemed to work for everyone who was there.

Ambassador College was such a very beautiful place to be, it was very well run, and we all had the freedom to enjoy the lovely campus grounds and the gardens. The very large grounds had a large boating lake, lovely buildings, the gardens themselves were really lovely with rose and Japanese gardens, and many other areas where you could sit and relax and enjoy yourself. It had a memorial hall, dormitories, and many classrooms, kitchens, a lovely music room that we could use whenever we wanted, it also had a gymnasium with an Olympic swimming pool, squash courts, a running track, and various other sports facilities for everyone who was there to enjoy.

Being in this lovely environment each day was beginning to change our lives, and these changes were definitely for the better. It was such a unique place to be, we were in an environment where everyone got on well, and they all worked for the good of everyone around them. To me, going to the campus was a bit like attending a stately home. I cannot imagine having a better time, or a nicer place to be going to each day.

Although it was your dad who was the student, I was able to take some of the classes with the other students. I really felt very much a part of what was happening there, as I was even allowed to have lunch in the student dining room on the days that I was there. I think that this was probably because I was the only student's wife who did not have children to look after, as your father had decided some time prior to this that he did not want us to have children.

As you can imagine, our life was suddenly very exciting for us. We didn't have time to have a dull moment during the time that we were there. There were many functions for us to attend, people to get to know, and many church families for us to visit with. We were kept very busy, as well as the college activities, we all met up every week with what I would think were about a thousand people for our services. We made many friends during the time that we were there. Some of whom are still our friends today! After being there for some time, I was so pleased to be able to do one of my very own favourite things, I was able to join one of the choirs.

Another nice thing happened to us at this time, several of the families who we were friendly with in the London church came up to the area to work at the college. This made it even nicer for us, as we were able to share the many events that they had there with many of our friends. Mr. Davis came to work at the college, and they as a family became a very significant part of our lives from then on.

Unlike most of the other students attending there, your father already had a degree, as he had his degree from Glasgow University. As a result of this he only had to complete three years of study at the college, in order to get the BA degree that he wanted.

Because we didn't have a lot of money at the time, it was suggested that I go to work in one of the departments at the college. I took a typing test there, and I failed this miserably as up until then I had not had any typing training. But everything worked out well for me in the end as they found me a job to do working in their mailing department. I really enjoyed working there and while I was there, I was given the opportunity to learn to type. This typing training has stood me in good stead throughout the rest of my life.

So you can imagine, we both soon settled in to our new lives at the college. Your dad seemed to love being there at the college, and we were at last on our way to a better future! We attended many of the classes, the meetings, field days, outings and in fact anything that we could while we were there.

We also spent a lot of our time with the lovely people who we were meeting, and everything seemed so good to me at the time. Many good changes seemed to be happening for us as a couple. Your dad was so different as there was no violence at all at this time of our lives. Your dad seemed very settled and happy with our lives, and I was very grateful for this change in him!

Yes, everything seemed so very good to me at this time!

So from then onwards, college life became the norm for us, if only I could really describe it to you! I could not have been any happier than at this lovely place. Everyone we met treated us so nicely, and we were happy and comfortable in our flat in Marshalswick. We certainly did have everything that we needed for us to be happy. When we were not working, we were able to socialise with all of the lovely people who were there at the college.

There were many exciting activities being held there at the college, we went to college dances, musical events, sometimes a wedding, student entertainment, they had a wonderful student choir and a very good church choir. It was always amazing to see the talent and the abilities of the many students who were attending there. I cannot speak for your father, but it truly was the best time of my entire life!

We were so very privileged, and as this first year continued, we got more and more involved, and as you know, tempus fugit, before we knew it and we could turn around, we had come to the end of the first college year.

In those first days at the college we were really struggling financially, it had not been a long time since your dad was attending the University in Glasgow, and we had not had the time to build up any resources. And now the year was nearing an end, and it looked very much as if we would have to have our holiday at home.

There weren't many married students at the college, but the year that your dad started there they had another married male student who had arrived there from South Africa with his beautiful wife and family. This man was already a doctor, but he was also taking a BA degree at Ambassador College.

I don't know how it came about, I know that your dad was friendly with him, as they were in the same class at the college, and he must have known that we were struggling to manage within our budget. When the college year was over, he and his wife very kindly asked us if we would like the opportunity of a continental holiday with them, they were planning to go away, and they had two seats available in their car.

How could we refuse such an amazing offer? So we said yes, that we would love to go with them. I think that this may have been our second year at the college (I'm not sure), because I know that at the time of the holiday I was expecting Ann, our first daughter. I know that we were at the college some time before we started having children! Yes, it was just before this holiday that we found out that I was having Ann, as I remember that every so often while we were travelling the doctor would stop the car for me to have a short walk to keep the blood circulating properly in my body. They were a lovely couple, and so very thoughtful!

On this trip that we had with them, we went to Holland for the first time in our lives. We were given accommodation when we got there by a member of their family who was a professional ballet dancer. She made us feel so welcome in her home, and I can remember that this was a very happy time for us. When we left there we travelled down through France and Germany. We went to Switzerland where we went up the Jungfrau Glacier on the cog railway.

This site is a UNESCO World Heritage site, and it is the highest railway station in Europe. From this site you can see as far as France and Germany. While we were on the top of the Jungfrau Glacier we visited and ate in the café, and we also went in to see the amazing Ice Palace. The views that we saw from the observation terrace would take your breath away.

I know that we must have stopped overnight somewhere, but I don't remember where this was. When we did leave the area, we continued on with our journey and we travelled through France and on until we reached Paris. We then stayed at a campsite in the centre of Paris, and it was from this camp site that we visited the famous Eiffel Tower. Because of my pregnancy I could not go up the tower that day, but your father did go to the top of the tower that day!

On our return from the holiday your father had to prepare himself for the following college year. And so we continued on with our lives, it was such a lot of fun for us during this time. The classes were really informative, and we continued to enjoy the various dances, sports events and the many other exciting activities that we could attend while we were there.

Like most other colleges and universities, they always had long summer breaks and Ambassador College was no exception to this!

On another of the college breaks, we got the opportunity to go with a party of students and one of the faculty members and his wife on an educational trip to Europe. We went through the Eastern part of Germany and into Berlin. This was at a time when the Berlin Wall was still in existence, and you could walk along the wall on the Western side and see the soldiers on the other side of the wall. The soldiers on the Eastern side of the wall were in their towers, they had their guns at the ready to be used as they thought was necessary!

We also went through Checkpoint Charlie while we were there in Germany, this was a rather amazing experience. We were able to see from the many pictures that they had there, the various things that the people would do to get themselves over the wall and so that they could escape from occupied East Germany. That day we drove through the Checkpoint and into East Germany, the car that I was travelling in that day had all of the foodstuffs that we were carrying in the boot of the car confiscated. The minibus that was with us had magazines and foodstuffs confiscated also on the way through the checkpoint. The guards were obviously concerned that we should not pass these on to the people who were living in the Eastern side of the wall.

While we were on this trip, we also went to visit the Dachau Concentration Camp site that was being run by the Americans. We saw yet again many photographs of the horrors that the people had gone through during the war. We walked on the ground that the prisoners had walked on, and then we went into the gas chambers, and after this we walked through to see the ovens where they put the people after they had killed them.

You can almost not believe that it is possible that such a place could have existed, never mind that it was used by anyone!

As you can see from the various things that we did while we were at the college, we had many opportunities to be fully immersed in college life, your dad was so well thought of and it really was an exciting place for anyone to be attending.

Being a member of the National Trust, I have recently been to a few of the beautiful stately homes that we have in this country. But suffice is to say, that being a part of Ambassador College life, was very much like being in the grounds of a stately home. The only difference is that we didn't have to leave after a short visit there!

Anyway, back down to earth again, and we continued to get on with our lives at the college. Each day your father would leave home and go on his way to attend his classes, and this life became the norm for us. Your father also continued teaching at the technical college in Watford to help us manage our finances.

After a period of time, we were asked if we would like to move to a maisonette in the Garston area of Watford; as this was nearer for your dad when he went to teach in the evenings. It was also obviously much better for us to be in a downstairs maisonette, now that we were having our first baby.

We realised that we needed to move again, we knew that this would be better for both of us, and for our little baby that I was having fairly soon. We moved there and we decorated it and we tried our best to make it a nice place to be living. When it was finished, it was a lot nicer than the flat that we had been living in Marshalswick, and we had the added advantage of a small garden at the back of the property. It also meant that we had some of our friends living near us, and this made it a lot nicer for us as a family.

Your dad had always said that he did not want to have children, but things changed for us in this different environment, as here we were waiting for the arrival of our first baby. I gave up my job at the college as I had to stay home during the day and prepare for the arrival of our first little daughter.

Our church friends were so very good to us, as I said previously we had limited funds at this time. Many of our friends turned up with various items for us, we were given a pram, a carry-cot, cot, clothes for the baby, blankets and in the end we had everything that we needed for the start of our baby's life. We had everything that we needed to make us happy and to help us at this time of our lives. When we were not working we were able to socialise and share many activities with the lovely people who were there.

Anyway the day finally arrived, we had obviously been preparing for some time, and here I was just about to give birth to our first baby. The delivery of our first daughter was not quite like I was expecting it to be. We had decided to have a home delivery and we had a midwife from the local hospital arrive at our home to deliver our baby. I seemed to be having what was an extremely long drawn out labour at the time. I am sure that every lady going through childbirth thinks this. I was pleased when it was all over and I was finally holding this my first little bundle in my arms. Ann my first daughter was born at last, and I was so proud of this little new addition to our family.

I can remember the first time that I put my daughter Ann into her pram, and I walked down the road with her. I was so excited, and I was such a proud mum. I do think that this is a pride that all women should enjoy, showing off their new baby to the outside world, and I was no exception to this! And it wasn't long before all three of us got used to living in our new home.

Now each year as was now our practice, we would go along in the autumn to our church convention. This year was going to be a bit different for us, as this year because I had just given birth to Ann I was unable to go to the festival. We asked my mum if she would come down to be with me, but because she could not come, your father's mother came to be with me while your dad went there by himself.

The convention was always the highlight of the year for us, as it was to us the most important time of the year. During our time away we spent time with many of the people that we had known throughout the year and also with some that we had not seen for some years. And because I couldn't go there this year, it was nice to hear the news from all of the people who returned afterwards.

I wasn't too disappointed that I could not go there that year; I had been given something that I could love and cherish for the rest of my life. I was so happy; I am sure that every new mother must love the time that she can share her new baby with everyone that she knows.

Your dad had obviously enjoyed being there at the convention, and when he came back home, he told me of the many good times that he had there, and about the many people that he had met while he was there. So he came back feeling refreshed and really excited about the next college year that was about to start.

So here we were once again, we were preparing ourselves for the commencement of the next college year that was about to start, and we were looking forward to the many exciting activities that would take place there.

Our friends who had been away at the festival told us of the wonderful time that they had had away, and it was nice catching up with everyone once again.

But having this little new baby became quite a challenge to us as a couple, as I am sure that it would be for any new mum and dad. We did everything that we could do to make her both comfortable and happy, but do you remember the first time that you breast fed your baby? Quite a challenge for any new mum and I was no exception to this!

As time went by, the three of us became what I thought was a nice little family. I was feeling so happy, and I would proudly show off my little Ann whenever we got the opportunity. And it seemed to me that everywhere that we took her, everyone seemed to like this little baby that we had just had. We continued going and meeting with our friends on a Saturday afternoon, and I was now able to join the mums in the area that they had there for attending to their babies.

The college year had started again, and a lot of things had changed for us, as we now had our little Ann to make arrangements for. Usually we both attended the social events, as wives were included in any that were held by the college. And at the time the family who we were the closest to us were our friends from London, and they were the Davis family. They for the most part were the family who helped us so that we could both attend the college functions. So you can tell from this, that early bonds were beginning to form between all of us.

Wives were always asked to attend these various functions, I think that this was because it was a co-ed college, and it was better for everyone if this happened.

And because we still had these functions to attend, we began to spend even more time in the company of the Davis family. Although they had several older children, they did not have any babies in their family at this time, and they were always willing to help us.

We had not long moved to our home in Garston, and our friends the Davis family lived in a really lovely detached house in Bricket Wood itself. Their house was fairly near to the college and it was on our route every time that we went to the college for college functions.

In fact your dad passed their house on his way to the college each day. And as it happened, the father of this family became your father's best friend, as you know, it is always good to have special friends to visit with. And as a result of this we started to share quite a lot of our time with them as a family.

Our home in Garston was a nice and convenient place for us to be at that time, as quite a number of the friends that we were making lived in the area. And now that I was based at home it was nice to be surrounded by our friends. I thought at the time that we were a happy couple!

We started to have some exciting times with our little daughter Ann, but it seemed that Ann was developing a very stubborn streak to her nature (I wonder who she got that from) very often at meal times both she and her father would do battle. This was especially if she did not want to eat the food that she was being given. Ann's father always had to have his way, and even at that very early age, they would have a fight going on between themselves, as they both wanted their own way; and Ann didn't give in too easily. I guess that this happens in all families with little ones, they really like you to know that they are there!

So we continued as one does, as you will know by now that we loved our time there at the college. We also loved the classes, the weekly meetings, the amazing social events. We enjoyed hearing the wonderful Ambassador chorale singing very many lovely songs. and we enjoyed seeing and getting to know the many students who we met there. There were always new people to get to know, and we really both enjoyed this.

During our time there at the college, we were friendly with a couple of the girl students who had come over from America to attend the college. They both seemed to love the time that they spent with us as a family. One of the young ladies, a really beautiful girl became a very special friend to both of us.

I think that you can tell from this, that I wasn't at all worried or concerned about the young ladies who attended the college, because at Ambassador College we were all like one big happy family!

As each day went by, we continued to be a part of what was going on at the college. I think that it was during this year that I took some of the classes myself, as I can remember getting up very early in the morning to get Ann organised for the day, as I was taking her to one of the other families while I was attending the class. I cannot describe what it was like to be there at this college, everyone loved being there, as you could not find anywhere nicer to spend your time.

So we continued with all of the events during the course of that college year, we didn't have any problems that year and before we knew where we were the year had come to an end, and we were getting ourselves ready for the formal ball at the end of the college year.

Anyway, you can tell that we had a good time, and after the ball was over etc..... we said our goodbyes to the students who were leaving and going back to their home countries once again. We knew that we would not see many of them again, and we also looked forward to the new intake of students who would come for the following year to the college.

We then began the preparation for another summer holiday, this time we decided that we would take a much needed trip to Scotland, as none of my family had met our daughter Ann. When she heard about this, our favourite American girl student asked if she could accompany us as she had always wanted to visit Scotland. She said that this would be a good opportunity for her as she planned to return to the United States the following year. We said yes, we were very happy to show her around some of Scotland, and we all prepared ourselves for the holiday.

So all four of us travelled to Scotland together, we spent our time touring around as one does while we were up there, we were especially concerned to make sure that our guest had a good time while we were there. We visited some of our family members and part of the time that we were up there we stayed on the Island of Millport. I think that when we got there that we hired some bikes and cycled around the island. After this we did a bit more sightseeing before we hit the road once more and headed back to England.

It turned out that this trip to Scotland was a huge success for all of us, and especially for the young

American lady who had accompanied us. She really enjoyed seeing the beautiful sights that she saw there in Bonnie Scotland!

For the rest of the summer we continued as usual with our family life, we were looking after our little daughter while at the same time we were socialising with the people who we were meeting. By this time the Davis family had become even closer friends of ours, so we spent our time socialising with them; and also the other people who we were meeting. The Davis family home in Bricket Wood was really lovely and it was always nice for us to spend our time with them, as they always had room in their house for a lot of visitors.

Now it was very near to this time that I realised that I was going to have another baby. I know that I only had about a year and four months between the ages of Ann and Grace, and Ann was going to be a year old in the autumn of that year.

Summer was flying by, and it wasn't long until we started to get ourselves ready for the autumn festival once again. Everyone who went there enjoyed these days when we would get together with our old and our new friends. We even had some visitors from overseas join us for these occasions, and we all thoroughly enjoyed these days together. Each family would usually stay in a chalet bungalow during the time that they were there, and the bungalows were prepared for us before we arrived at the site. During the time that we were there, we would share the wonderful times and the activities that had been organised for us.

When we went this year we had our little Ann to take with us for the first time, and in addition we also had another baby on the way. And so our preparations were very different this year for us. But in fact, everything went quite smoothly for us, we arrived in plenty of time and got ourselves booked in. This particular year the site had an open plan dining room for all of the families to eat in. The room was very well organised, much like a very large canteen, and this made it especially nice for families like us. It meant that mums didn't have to spend a lot of time preparing meals for their own families. What a brilliant idea for everyone!

I particularly enjoyed these times, we hadn't had any holidays when I grew up in my family, and so I really appreciated these times when we could attend this lovely event. This time we had our own little daughter Ann with us, and this made it even more enjoyable for us. Our Ann was around one year old by this time, and it was on this particular occasion when we were there at the festival that we spent a lot of our time with the Davis family. Nothing wrong with this, we knew them really well as they often looked after our little daughter Ann when we attended any college functions!

During this time that we had away, we spent a lot of our time with the Davis family as they helped us with Ann as she could be quite stubborn at times. It was during this time however, that I noticed that your dad seemed to have a particular interest in the youngest daughter of the Davis family. Perhaps this was happening because she was helping me with our daughter Ann. Perhaps I noticed it because I was his wife, and possibly because of our life in the past.

But it was there at the festival that I really became aware of this interest!

I know that my daughters will probably think that I am strange, why would I notice this or even think about this! You know by now that we as people are all very friendly towards each other, and it was very early on in our friendship with this family. Her parents were a little bit older than we were, they already had five children, two of whom had grown up and left home by this time.

So you will realise why I pushed this thought to one side in my head, I told myself that I was even silly to notice this! But I did discuss it with your dad, and he told me that she had overheard a conversation between her parents and one of our elders. They were apparently talking about both herself and her brother; and she told your dad that she did not like what she had heard them talking about; and that as a result of this she was very unhappy and resentful of her parents. And since then, unknown to me she was apparently confiding in your dad!

During a discussion that we had, your dad said that he wanted to help her as he felt sorry for her! And I think that this may have been the beginning part of what eventually happened to our family.

Yes, I am actually embarrassed here in telling you this, there is no way that this should have concerned me, my daughter Ann was only a one-year old baby at this time. I was carrying Grace at the time and I started to carry Grace before Ann was one-year old. But this was certainly before Grace was born. So I think that you will understand why I put this out of my thoughts, I thought that I was even silly to notice the attention that he seemed to be giving her as this girl was so very young at the time.

Nothing should have crossed my mind about their friendship!

So we all continued to enjoy the activities that they had there for us, nothing should spoil our time there, as I said it was the highlight of our year. And when the festival was over we returned home again just in time for the commencement of the following year at the college.

Back home again and on with our usual routine, and as I said to you Ann our daughter continued to be a fairly stubborn child when she was very little, and there was usually a war of wills going on between her and her father. Usually they both wanted to have their own way, and this made it difficult at times for us. Most of the time I was pre-occupied and it was just as well, as it always upset me when (as her dad thought) our little daughter had to be corrected. As far as I was concerned, the punishment that he inflicted far outweighed whatever the problem was, but her daddy always as usual got the last word on this.

I think that my husband always wanted his young daughter to behave perfectly, (just like he did?) or at least he wanted her to do just what he wanted her to do! This was typical of him, he always had to have things his way, and Ann had to learn this!

Your father was doing really well at Ambassador College. During his time there he built the weather satellite station, and this was in addition to the other duties that he had there. From the weather station he prepared weather forecasts for both the Guardian newspaper and the Yachting and Boating Magazine. The satellite station was located on the college campus. I think that in addition to this there was an observation tower located nearby. He was also a ham operator, and he would spend a lot of his spare time speaking to other ham operators all around the world.

I know that he loved the work that he did there at the college, he would tell me of the things that he was doing, and I was really happy to be involved in whatever it was that he wanted me to do, it was important to me that he was able to use all of his skills. As you can tell, our lives were so very full during the time that we were there. Perhaps he was just too clever, he was doing so well, and he must have thought that he could do anything that he wanted! We seemed to have so much going for us at this time, no-one could blame him for being pleased about how he was doing!

As you know, I was carrying Grace around this time, someone had told me that you wouldn't get pregnant when you were breast-feeding a baby. But I am pleased to say that this is not true, because it was during the time that I was breast feeding Ann that I got pregnant with Grace, my second daughter. Sometimes these things happen when you least expect them, but what a lovely surprise!

So once again we started to prepare ourselves for our next new arrival, we were now experienced parents, or so we thought at the time! This little baby should be a lot easier to have and manage than Ann was, and it turned out that we were right in thinking this, as our daughter Grace had a lovely temperament from the moment that she was born, and she was always such a happy child!

Anyway as you normally do, we prepared everything ready, just as we had done the first time when we had Ann, but by this time we knew that we were going to be a bit overcrowded in our little maisonette. It was at this time that we thought that we should try to move again!

Now we had decided again to have another home delivery for our baby, and Grace our second daughter was born in the same maisonette in Garston as our daughter Ann. She was delivered that day by a lovely Indian nurse, the nurse was the college nurse, and she was such a lovely person. Everything went well for us that day, the delivery happened so very quickly, and after it was over, we decided to call our new baby daughter Grace, after the nurse who delivered her.

And of course, you can imagine the delight that I had the first day that I walked my two babies out from our home in Garston. Baby Grace was lying in the pram and Ann was on a seat on the top of the pram, and I proudly walked them down to the shops. I was very much hoping that someone would notice me with my two little daughters!

So here we were, we were gradually increasing our family, your dad was still at the college as a student, and it seemed that most things seemed to be running along smoothly for both of us. All we had to do from this time onwards was to continue with our routine and everything would be all right for us in the future!

Now I don't know who arranged it; but I know that it was some time after this; that I was told that the Davis's youngest daughter needed some extra tuition to help her with her school work. And at the time that I was told this, it was arranged that she come over to our home in Garston for one evening a week, as she was going to have this tuition from your father.

147

And so this was when the visits started, and they continued for many years after this. And during the time that she was there for her studies, the girl started helping me with Ann and Grace. She seemed to love spending her time there with us, and she seemed to be really fond of our children!

I can say at this point, that I was very happy with this arrangement. We were the best of friends with her parents, and your dad and I were becoming very fond of the girl. She in turn loved to come over to us, as she loved being with our little daughters. It seemed to be an arrangement that suited both families, as we were spending a lot of our spare time with them as a family. They often invited us to their home on a Saturday for a meal in the evening after we had been to the campus.

So she started to come over regularly on a Tuesday evening from this time on, and in the morning your father would drop her off at Imperial School on his way to the college for his work. And so this arrangement that they had for her homework continued from this time onwards, and was still happening until the time that they ran away together!

It was sometime after this; I know that it was when we were still living in the Garston maisonette, that we heard that they were looking for new members to join the church choir. And you know, one of my favourite things is to sing! I know that I would not have left a new baby so I think that Grace must have been quite manageable by this time. And so after thinking about if it would work for us as a family, I joined the church choir.

Just by coincidence the choir was on the same evening that the young girl came over for her studies, but in spite of this it was decided that I should go to the rehearsal that they held at the college. I was accepted in the choir, and I felt very privileged to be in it!

And so our routine changed for us on a Tuesday evening. I fed and bathed the children as I wanted them to be happy and settled before I left. Your father would pick the girl up on his way home from the college and the five of us would have some dinner together. Afterwards we would all spend some time with the children before they were put to bed for the evening. Afterwards I would leave home and drive myself to the college for the rehearsal. During the time that I was away, your father would help the girl with her homework.

Now I don't know the length of time that this continued for, but this was happening for quite a long time, and of course I did notice that your dad and the girl were becoming very attached to each other; but you know, she was a very young schoolgirl at the time. Yes, I did bring the subject up with your dad on several occasions, and the reply that I got was the usual one. I was jealous and worrying over nothing, and you know for some reason I hated being told that I was jealous, it was to me as if it were the worst sin in the world! Perhaps your dad knew this, and he played on this and took advantage of my weakness with this.

I really loved going to the choir practice, even although the choir director at the time found my voice too Scottish to do any of the solos, I could still help with the general choir work. So I really enjoyed my evenings out for the rehearsal that we had, and I continued going there each week.

I can honestly say that I cannot remember the age the girl was at this time, all I do know was that she was a very young schoolgirl at the time, my own two daughters were still very little and in fact I still thought of them as babies at this time.

Now this to the best of my ability is the fact about this, I am not excusing myself in any way! You will ask me why I let something like this happen in my home. Apart from your father, I had no male influence in my life. I didn't know then that some men schooled girls! I realise it now, but I did not realise it at that time of my life.

I grew up with a mum and three sisters, we did not talk about things like this in our home and the only influence that I had was your father. If I questioned him about this, I was always in the wrong for thinking that anything could be wrong in their friendship!

So yes, I was young and foolish, and much too trusting as a person. Something else I would like you to think about is that we were at a religious college and it was your father who was the student. He was the one who pushed to go there. He was attending classes that taught him how to conduct his life properly, and from people who really understood people and human nature. I fully accepted in my mind at the time that your father was being true to what he was learning during the time that we were there.

It is true that alarm bells were beginning to ring in my head, but when they rang and I asked your dad, he always said that I was wrong to be concerned, and he would accuse me of being jealous of the young girl.

Anyway I am going to continue with the rest of the story, as I must tell you of an incident that happened that made me start to get worried about things.

So the first time that anything happened that I am aware of, was one of the nights that I had to go to the choir. We were still living in our home in Garston at the time, and it was a night when I was going out for another choir rehearsal.

I got myself organised as usual, and with dinner over and my babies safely tucked up in bed for the night, I left home and I drove myself to the college to meet up with the other choir members. But when I arrived there that evening, I discovered much to my surprise that the choir rehearsal had been cancelled for the evening. So completely unsuspecting of anything, and because I believed and trusted in this man that I had married, I was surprised at what happened when I arrived home that evening.

So I drove myself back home, I pulled the car up outside of our home. In the house where we were living at the time that this occurred, we had a big picture window in our lounge, and consequently we had venetian blinds at the window. Now when I arrived back home that evening, I was surprised to see that the venetian blinds were drawn and that the house seemed to be in darkness.

Now when I saw this, I think that I must have frozen on the spot. I didn't know how to react to this, or even what to do! So far as I knew, your dad and the girl were intended to be studying for her school, why then would the room be in darkness?

I think that when I saw the blinds drawn that I was a bit scared that evening, and I wondered what I might find there! I had always been afraid of your dad, and I was always wary of upsetting him. I hadn't thought for a minute that I couldn't trust him, especially since we had come to the college.

Neither had I thought at any time that I should stay home while the girl was there, he was living this new way of life that we were learning about at the college, and I really believed that he was as fully immersed in it as I was. And it had been a long time since I had to have the results of his anger.

But I must admit to you that I walked up the drive to our home that evening, and although I did not want to, I knew that I had to go in to the house. This was my home, and I opened the outside door that evening with much fear and trepidation.

Here I was once again, having to wonder about what was going on in our lives, and in my own home. So if you could imagine my feelings, when I walked up and I opened the door of our home that evening, yes, I was quite afraid of what I might find on the other side of the door.

But yes, I plucked up the courage and I did go in. I put my key into the door-lock and I entered, and much to my surprise your father came out of the darkened lounge; he met me in the hallway and he took hold of my arm and guided me through and into our bedroom. I asked him what was happening and he gave me some reason why the room was in darkness at the time. He said that he hadn't heard the car come back and he assured me that nothing was wrong, and that I should not worried about anything.

Now as you can tell, and as I now know, I have been naïve, but I loved your dad, and the violent times in our marriage had stopped, we were at a religious college and I fully believed that he was following the things that we were being taught!

Hand in heart, I did really believe him at the time, I believed that I was making something out of nothing, when your dad gave me his explanation that evening.

But sadly for our family it did not end there!

After this incident, things seemed to me to be just normal for us as a family. Your dad went to the college each day as he usually did, and he even managed to get some work to do on the campus to earn some more money for us. It wasn't long after this that he was able to give up the teaching job that he had at the Watford Technical College. He was making good progress towards his BA degree and the young girl became like a part of our family. From this time onwards because the girl knew the children so well, she would come over and baby-sit for us whenever we attended the various college functions. She became a regular visitor to our home and everyone who was involved, including her parents, who seemed to be really happy about this.

Everyone seemed to love our little girls, they were such lovely little children, and we were so very proud of them, as they were healthy and happy and such fun to be with. The only problem we had was between Ann and her dad, as there was often a battle of wills going on between them, and this happened quite frequently for us! Now Grace was very different in her temperament to Ann, she was so easy to manage right from the moment that she was born. You couldn't help but love this little child, and her dad seemed to have a special liking for her.

Now this arrangement that we had with the girl, and of course with her parents' approval continued from this time onwards. And because it became a part of our regular routine everyone seemed to be going along quite happily. But - yes, there is always a 'but', isn't there - I think that you were possibly expecting it! The answer was of course, I was not, I was the only one who was not always happy with the situation, but everyone else was, and I felt compelled to accept it!

After this event we carried on with our lives as if nothing had happened. Your father was doing so well as he now had full time work at the college, and this meant that we could manage better as a family. He was making good progress with his college work in preparation for the BA degree, and it seemed as if everyone was happy except me!

During all of this time we were still living in the maisonette in Garston, but because we were rather overcrowded there, it was decided then that it would be better for your dad if he lived nearer to the college!

Your dad's younger sister and his mum

Chapter 8
He Was Always One Step Ahead of Me

After this incident was over, we put it behind us and we carried on as if nothing had happened. At the time I accepted your father's explanation, I was paranoid wasn't I? He said that I was jealous and looking for something that didn't exist!

Perhaps because your father was doing so well at the college; after all we were attending a religious college at this time; I fully believed what your dad said. And the result of this was that I went along with whatever it was that he told me.

From this time onwards your dad was given some full-time work at the college. And this work would help to provide for us during our time there. He was also making such good progress with the studies that he was doing for his degree; everyone who was involved with him at the time seemed very happy with what he was doing. The young girl had become like a part of our family, and it seemed to me that she was always with us.

During our time at the college we were both very busy people, we both had a lot of social events to attend, and this always kept us on our toes, in addition to this we had our little family to look after and care for. We seemed very fortunate at the time to have our friends' young daughter to help us with our children, and so we continued on like this, enjoying the special time that we were having there at the college.

As I said before, the maisonette was a bit on the small side for our growing family, and because of this your dad spoke to the man in charge of rented properties at the college. He asked him if he could find us another property that we could live in. And this worked out really well for us, as he managed to find us another property and it was situated much nearer to the college, as it was in Bricket Wood itself. The house was a lovely detached house, and because it was nearer to the campus we only had a short drive from there to our new home.

Our new house was fairly large, it was detached and it had three good sized bedrooms and a main lounge. It also had a second lounge adjoining the main lounge, and this had been added later as an extension. It also had a large and lovely kitchen, a dining room, upstairs bathroom and downstairs toilet, and it had a most beautiful garden. The house was amazing inside, as it was more than anything that we could possibly need or even hope for as a family.

Who would ever have thought it possible that we would have such a nice home as this one was to live in? It was much better than any other house that either of us had ever lived in during our entire lives. Anyway we started our packing, organised the children, and after everything was done, we made the move from Garston, and into our new home in Bricket Wood.

This house that we were moving to was a really lovely home for us. And it was in a really nice neighbourhood for our little children to grow up in. We loved it there, we had many friends living nearby, and we were so near to the college that we could invite the students over to visit with us. We started to do a lot of entertaining when we moved to this house, and the Davis family who were our best friends, and the people who we spent the most of our time with, also lived much nearer to us here. As a result of this we were able to socialize a lot more, both with them and with other families who lived near to us.

One of the things that we started to do when we went to this house, was to go on a Saturday evening to the gymnasium and watch various teams playing basketball. Our little daughter Ann, who was now a toddler, used to join the girls who were the cheerleaders for the game that they were playing. Ann would try her best to copy the various moves that the girls were doing to cheer the men on. It was quite funny to see a little toddler doing this!

So we spent a lot of our time enjoying this lovely house and the many people who came over to see us. Sometime later, and while we were living in this lovely house, your father graduated from the college and he then had his BA degree to add to his other degree and letters.

Graduation day was always a very exciting time for everyone. My babies were looked after by the mother of the Davis family while this was going on, as her daughter would have been at school at the time. The weather that day was hot and sunny and so very lovely, they always held the event at that time of year after the students had completed another year of their studies, and of course those in their final year would be graduating and finishing their training and returning to their various homes once again.

The graduation ceremony was a really lovely social event, almost like a large wedding, and everyone was feeling as happy as they should on that day. Many of the students who were attending the college had come to the college from various other countries around the world, and they would be looking forward to returning home again after such an exciting event.

We arrived there that day wondering what the day would bring for us of course, we knew that your dad would graduate that day, but at the time we hadn't made any plans for the future.

The day started with an amazing brunch that was being held in the college grounds just outside of memorial hall. The many students had done an amazing job of making the area look very inviting for the occasion. And it seemed that people had been really busy as we also had some lovely food to eat. We sat there with some of the students who were our friends by this time, and I think that we had one faculty member sitting at our table with us that day. After all of the food was over, we would have spent some time talking and visiting with one another. We were all very happy and enjoying the time, and we were glad that we could spend some more time getting to know each other better. We had such a lovely time there, and it was after this that the graduation ceremony began.

And here he was, after all of his hard work, your father was standing up there on the platform. I watched as he received his Bachelors of Arts degree that day, and this was to add to his BSc degree that he already had from Glasgow University. What an amazing achievement that was for him that day, he must have felt really wonderful, as I am sure all of the other students felt that day. After the ceremony was over, everyone congratulated all of the students on their wonderful achievements. You know that remembering this event makes me even more aware as a person, of what a great privilege it was that we were there at the college as a family.

I think that as well as the graduation ceremony that they held that day, they also had a couple of weddings on that day. They were held on the college campus, as they were held in one of the buildings that they had there, and then the receptions for these were held in the lovely grounds that they had at Ambassador College.

Anyway the day (as they all do) came to an end all too quickly, and many of the friends that we had known for some years by now, went back to their homes and to the areas that they had come from.

Now after the graduation ceremony and other exciting events were over, we carried on with our lives just as we normally did, but with yet another big thing happening for us as a family. Suddenly your father was promoted, and he was now a member of the Faculty of Ambassador College. Who would ever have believed that this was possible? We came from very humble beginnings, and now we had this amazing honour bestowed upon us.

And this was then, the beginning of your father's teaching career at the college!

After this we went on another summer holiday that year. I can't remember which of the holidays this was, what I do know, was that each year we went away during the summer break. We always needed this time to prepare ourselves for the following year at college, and we were already very excited about what would happen that next year. It was going to be even more exciting for us than ever, as your dad would be teaching there at the college for the very first time.

Up until this time, we had had to struggle quite a bit financially to pay our way, but because your dad was now going to be on the teaching staff, this would mean that he would have a teacher's salary for us to live on, and of course this meant that we would have a much better income to support ourselves and our little family.

This summer after a short time away, we spent more of our time at home. I think that it would have been around this time that your father built the weather satellite station at the college. And at the time we continued having many visitors come to our home to visit with us. We had never had it as good as this was, and we were beginning to get settled into our new home.

Socialising was one of the things that we both enjoyed, and it wasn't long before the students were arriving back from their summer holiday, and they started to get themselves organised for the beginning of another college year. We really enjoyed sharing our time with others, and we would often invite some of the students over for dinner and an evening of music and dancing. We had the room where we were living, and everyone always seemed to enjoy the time that they spent with us, and our little family.

The young American girl who we were particularly friendly with (you will remember that we took her to Scotland) would often come over to our home during the week when your dad was away doing his work at the college. She said that she liked to be in someone's home, as it reminded her of her own home in the States; she said that it was good to get a break from being in a dormitory at the college. The children and I always enjoyed the days that she came over.

I can remember this summer quite well, the weather was really lovely, and we were able to spend quite a lot of our time that year, both enjoying our lovely garden, and also our house and all of the people who came to visit with us!

And during all of this time, we were continuing to be visited by our young babysitter, your father's best friend's daughter, as she now lived fairly near to us in this house. And it is perhaps because we were having so many people around (including young female students) to our home, and we were all having such a good time, that it seemed silly for me to be concerned about this little underage girl, even although it seemed to me that she was always hanging around with us.

The girl always loved to come to our home, and she would spend as much time as she could with our children. As I said, by now we only lived a short distance away from her parents, and this is probably the reason that she spent so much of her time with us. Your dad was now a part of the college faculty, and there were even more activities for us to attend at the college, and the young girl was always happy to look after our children for us.

So what could possibly go wrong for us?

Now when we were in this house, we had many visits from rather stunning young girl college students, including the one who we took to Scotland with us, and we were also very friendly with many of the young men who were there. Some of them thought of our home as a home from home. Why then, would anyone think that I should be concerned about this young schoolgirl who was coming over to be with our family? As she was there helping us with our children.

But because of the changes that were happening within our family at this time, my own personal worries seemed rather silly, as the girl was so very young at the time.

But as time went by, I did begin to get more and more concerned about her visits. I again spoke to your father, and again he said that there was nothing wrong, and that I was worrying about nothing. But then as things developed further I started to get even more worried about her visits, as she seemed to be able to twist your father around her little finger during any of the times that she was there with us!

But silly me, I was always very controlled by your dad. Any time that I spoke to your dad about it, I was the one who was wrong. Wives should submit to their husbands, and this was the law in our family. Your father always played an ace on this, as if he wasn't enough of a bully already!

But it still seemed to me at the time, very much as if the girl was taking over my family!

And as you all know, of course she did!

When I think about it now, what were her parents thinking of? They only lived within a short walking distance of us at the time, why did she always have to stay overnight with us? Didn't her parents have any suspicions at all? They saw your father and the girl together, they were obviously backwards and forwards a lot of times between both of our family homes together. Surely her parents must have wondered at times, and considered that something wrong may be happening between them?

Was I to be the only responsible person here in this? No-one asked me at any time what I thought, or even what I wanted during all the time that this was happening in our lives. This girl, as young as she was, was having a very bad influence on our family, but her parents continued to let her come over to our house for her studies, and they even let her stay the night regularly with us, even although their home was but a short distance away at the time.

I am sure that there is no other schoolgirl in the whole of the country who has had as many years of help with their school work as she seemed to need!

Why didn't her parents get even a little bit suspicious, and start to ask them questions?

I particularly remember this time that I am going to try to describe to you, it was the first time that I actually began to think that they were both fooling me, and that something may in fact be happening between them. I was being asked and expected to think that their relationship was completely harmless, but the first time that I really had my doubts, and was nearly convinced that I was right, was a night when she stayed over with us once again.

They both arrived at our home together on one of the evenings, your father had picked her up on his way home, and we all sat together and had our family dinner that evening. After dinner there would be some fun with the children that we would all enjoy, and then I would take the children upstairs and get them bathed and ready for bed. Afterwards the children came downstairs again to say their goodnights and to have their hugs etc., and later while I was putting them to bed, your father and the babysitter would sit down together in our sitting room and they would start doing her studies. A little bit later, after the children were tucked up safely in bed for the night, I would come back down the stairs, clear up the kitchen area, and join them both in the sitting room.

One of the things that I enjoyed the most in the evenings in our home was that your dad always played some lovely music for us to listen to. I remember going on one occasion with your father to the music room at the college, and we spent the evening recording some of the music that they had there. It was almost like a tradition in our home, to have music on in the background in the evenings.

It was good to know that our children were happy, and that they were safely tucked up in bed, and that at last, I had got over the hustle and bustle of the day. I was by this time tired and looking forward to sharing a relaxing evening with your father, while we listened to some of our music.

As I mentioned before, we had two sitting rooms in this house, and we didn't use the second one very much at all, as even with two young children, it was a little bit surplus to our requirements. But when our babysitter stayed over, this was the room that she would sleep in. The room had a really large settee, and this was usually where the girl slept when she came over to stay the night with us!

As the evening drew in, your father and the young girl finished the homework that she had to do. She told us that she was going to bed, and she said her goodnights to us. Your father and I continued sitting there, as at the time we were listening to our nice music, and talking together.

A short time later, and much to my surprise, the door of the second sitting room opened once again. By this time, I would have expected that the young babysitter would have been asleep. But when she came through the doorway, she walked over to where we were sitting, and much to my surprise and shock, she was dressed in a see through grown up type of nightdress. The next moment she came over to us, and she gave us both a goodnight kiss. I was not sure at all how I should react at the time, because I knew that if I asked your father about it, and complained to him, he would just get angry with me. And so this was done and accepted as if it were quite normal in our house.

The following morning after they left our home; the routine was that your dad would drop the girl off at Imperial School for her school day, and afterwards he would go on to the college for his own day's work.

I can remember the day quite well, a friend was visiting later to spend some time with both me and the children, and I had to start getting things ready for her visit. Not so much now, but in those days I was very particular about cleanliness (too much so), and I wanted everything to be spic and span before she arrived that afternoon. So I did my usual chores, our own bedroom first, and then I got the children up and ready for the day ahead. I then left them playing while I tidied their room, then I did any of the other things that needed to be done in the upstairs part of the house.

I worked my way through the downstairs part of the house. Our house was really lovely and easy for me look after at the time, and I had left the room that the girl slept in as the last one to do. It was then time to tidy up this second living room. It was when I was clearing up her bedding that I discovered that the bed settee that she had been sleeping on was soaking wet. And I must admit that I was a little bit curious about this.

I continued getting myself organised however, and we all had a most lovely day with our visitors.

But I couldn't see any explanation for the wet settee, and because I was obviously curious about it, when I asked your dad about it later, he explained it away by telling me that her hot water bottle had burst in the night, and of course I had no alternative but to accept this explanation from him. As I said previously, I was sure that he was just as committed as I was to this new way of life that we were meant to be living.

Anyway, there was nothing more said about this incident, either then at that time, or even later.

I know now that I was obviously fooled once again!

But unfortunately as it happened, from this time onwards, your father did not try to hide his interest in the young girl from me, or she in him. It was as if I wasn't there with them any more. And the only exception to this was, if I asked something that he did not like, he would start to get angry and violent again towards me. So once again I was living in a situation where I was not allowed to question anything at all that either one of them was doing, as he would always get angry with me if I did.

As I told you before, I was always afraid of your father, right from the very beginning of our marriage, and I was afraid of the things that he was prepared to do to get his own way. This girl was so young, and if I questioned them about anything I was always in the wrong for asking. And so you will be able to understand, that I became increasingly concerned, as they were starting to gang up together against me any time that she was there. And if she wanted to have the children, your dad would take them away from me and give them to her.

It was around this time that we had our second visit from your father's mum from Scotland. We had already lost your grandfather, and so it was nice of your grandmother to travel all the way down to see us from Scotland. She thought that our Ann and Grace were such lovely children. You will remember that I told you before, that your grandmother on your father's side had refused to come to our wedding. And she was also very good at stirring up trouble for both us, and for the other members of the family after we got married. So this journey to see us was only her second visit to see us. It was your grandmother who had come to be with me, when your dad went to the festival, just after I had given birth to Ann. At that time my own mother was asked, but she could not come.

But on this visit, during the time that she was there, we had visits from this little girl who was our baby-sitter, and this seemed to bother her quite a lot. Perhaps it brought back memories of a possibility in the past to her at that time?

But even so, your grandmother seemed to be very happy to be there with us, and she said that our two little daughters were really lovely, but of course she would have been biased as they were her granddaughters. And at the time, I was especially pleased that she enjoyed being there with me, and this was because of the rejection that I had received from her when we got married. She also said a very nice thing to me during that visit, she said that I was a better wife to her son than he was a husband to me.

She really did enjoy spending her time with us, and she made her peace with me at that time!

So it was very nice for me to have that accolade from her!

I am not sure just how long your grandmother stayed with us on that holiday, but I know that it became time for us to prepare ourselves to travel once again to the next yearly convention. I asked your dad if his mum could come with us, but he didn't want this, and so I then suggested that she stay there until we returned home again. But again your father was not happy with this idea either. So he arranged to take her to catch the train for Scotland before we left. I am certain though that she left us under a cloud at that time. I knew that she was not happy on the day that she left us, perhaps it was that she saw something that she was concerned about while she was there?

I also think that when she left us, that both she and your dad had had some words. But sadly however, this was the last time we saw her. I know that she made it back to Scotland, because she arrived at her daughter's house in Gilmerton in rather a bad state of mind. Apparently she started to cause a lot of trouble there with them very soon after she arrived there. The end result of this was that her son-in-law had to have her hospitalised, and it was while she was there in the hospital that she died.

We had spent our time at the festival enjoying all of the lovely food, and also the many activities that were usually organised for everyone while we were there. And it was always so good to see the friends that we had not seen for the last year. We had a wonderful time there, and it didn't seem long until we had to return back home once again and get ourselves ready for yet another college year.

Sometime after we returned from the festival, we were informed of what had happening up there in Scotland. It sounded as if your grandmother was hospitalised during the time that we were at the convention. We were told afterwards about the trauma that she caused there, and this was just after she had visited with us at our home in Bricket Wood.

So you can imagine what a shock it was, when we heard of the news of your grandmother's death on our arrival back from the festival. We were told that when she arrived in Scotland, that she had to be put into the hospital, both for her own sake, and for the safety of others. This was because she was causing major problems at her daughter's house, and it was while she was being treated in the hospital, that she had died a short time later.

It was very sad for us to hear of her death like that, and naturally your father was very upset, as he had just lost his mum. The only thing that your father wanted to do after hearing this bad news was to leave immediately for Scotland. He wanted to do what he could to help with the funeral arrangements, as these were already being made by his sister.

So once again, we left our daughters Ann and Grace with the Davis family, while we went up there to Scotland to attend your grandmother's funeral.

It was during the time that we were there in Scotland that your dad and his sister had the first quarrel that I have known them to have. It was a really big quarrel, and I know that they were both really upset. It was really sad to see this happen, as they were both so extremely fond of each other.

I was later told by your dad that the row that they had was because he and his sister had disagreed with each other about the music for the funeral, and that they had also disagreed about the other arrangements that had already been made for the funeral before we arrived there. I have sometimes wondered if this could have been the real reason for such a big row as they had. Also at the same time, your aunt refused point blank to come to the family home in Bellsmyre and help us clear out the property.

So as it happened, after the funeral was over we travelled by ourselves to Bellsmyre to do this. And whatever the row was about, I really do not know! But you know your dad yourselves, he always has to have things just the way he wants them. I think that this quarrel was never resolved between them after this. I know that your aunt is dead now, but I do not know if your dad ever contacted her again, as so very many things happened in our own lives from this time onwards.

But because your aunt refused to help us, your father and I went to Bellsmyre by ourselves, and we did all of the necessary things that had to be done there, as we had to leave the house empty before we could return to the college again. So we organised for the furniture to be taken to one of the charities, we cleared out all of the clothing that was still in the house, and we sorted the bedding. All of the papers that we found were burned by your father in the garden, and almost everything else in the house was given to one of the local charities. We brought home a very few items in the car, and one small item of furniture that your dad had made when he was at school, was put into a neighbour's loft to be collected later, and I don't know if this was ever collected by him.

After we dealt with everything in Scotland, we travelled back to the college area to pick up our children, and to get on with the next college year. So here we were, once again back into the same routine again, your dad was teaching physical sciences and some other subjects at the college. We heard when we returned to the college that they wanted their masters to be as qualified as possible, (something to do with college accreditation) and your father was offered the opportunity to have a day out each week to do a PHD degree at London University.

But all during this time I was getting increasingly aware that we had a big problem over our babysitter. Your dad was always so clever, and the young girl I was worried about was so very young at the time, that I should not have had to be concerned about their friendship. But she could do no wrong, she always had to come first in our house. She not only came occasionally but she started being with us most of the time, both at home and when we were out with others.

What were her parents thinking about?

But no matter how I felt, they both continued to gang up on me, and I seemed to be the only one who was unhappy with the way they were both behaving. Her parents were very happy about the arrangement that they had for their daughter, and I seemed to be the only person who had a problem with it.

So we were continuing to get on with our lives, and here I was, in spite of the problems that we were having, I discovered that I was pregnant once again. This was another surprise for me, considering that your dad and I had this major problem going on in the background of our lives. But sorry Joy, perhaps this was just to side-track me and keep me busy, and so that I would not notice the things that were going on between your dad and the girl. I will never know the answer to this!

And when I heard this news, I was thrilled at the prospect of having another baby!

During the ensuing months though, things were happening to make me very worried at home. Some of the times when the girl was there, your father would take Ann and Grace away from me and give them to the young girl. There was no medical reason for this to happen to us, as I was always very well during the time that I was pregnant. They both knew that I wasn't happy about this, and that I was unhappy about their friendship, but all of the time your father just wanted to please the girl. It was obvious to me, that he was taking sides between us and changing the goalposts in our family.

So as usual I attended all of the normal medical check-ups, and fortunately everything seemed to be quite normal with the pregnancy, and the medical team were happy that all would be well with both me and the birth of the baby. It meant though that I was kept really busy from then on, as I had all of the preparation work to do for the arrival of our baby. At the time your dad was either working, or he was studying for his PHD. And when not doing these things, he was obsessed in his friendship with the young girl, even although he was telling me that there was nothing for me to be worried about.

Now it was approximately three months later when your father arrived home and he told me that we had been asked to chaperone a group of students to go on a field trip to Majorca. He really wanted to go on this trip, and usually when officials went on these trips, they were expected to be accompanied by their wives, and this meant that I was to also go on this trip with them. So he talked to me about it at home, and we decided that we would go on the trip even although I was carrying Joy at the time. He organised this with the other people involved, and sometime later on, he told me that he wanted to take the young babysitter on the trip with us.

As you can imagine, from the things that I have said previously, I was really unhappy about this idea. And at the time I said that she was not accompanying us on the trip.

Now you could say that this was a big mistake on my part, your father had been very violent to me in the past before we went to the college, and he was again showing signs of anger and aggressiveness towards me, and

175

especially if I did not do just what he wanted. He always insisted in getting his own way, and this time was no exception.

This discussion was going on in our bedroom, and he grabbed me and pushed me down on to the bed, and in spite of the fact that I was carrying his baby, he took a child's wooden paddle that we kept in the house (this was like very a small cricket bat), and he started paddling me with this. I had really angered him, and when I still refused to take the girl with us, he continued until I was bruised from my waist down to the top of my legs.

He asked me once again, he was fully expecting that I would give in to him and agree that she could go with us, but this time I would not give in to him. I was determined at the time that I would not go on holiday with the girl, and as a result of this, he was forced to go on the holiday without her. Once again we arranged for the Davis family to look after our two little daughters, and we were then on our way to Majorca with the group of college students to look after.

When I think about it now, we were not really suitable people to be looking after a group of young students, as our own life was in such a mess at this time!

So bruises and all, we arrived for the holiday in Majorca, we stayed in a lovely hotel accompanied by about twelve students from the college. None of them saw any of the bruising that I had on my body, or knew anything about the problems that we were having at home. It is so strange, that not one person ever said anything to me about the friendship that your dad had with the girl. But I was told afterwards that the girl was seen regularly at the weather satellite station where your dad worked, and no-one thought anything at all about this, either about her being there, or about them spending so much time together.

While we were away on this trip to Majorca, we did have one very unfortunate incident, and I would have thought that some of the students must have started wondering about both our marriage, and about our relationship. Interestingly at a festival some years later, I met an American man who told me that his daughter who was on that trip, had told him about the condition that I was in while we were on that holiday. So it was noticed, but no-one said anything about it.

I thought that the Majorca trip was going very well for everyone, or so it seemed to me. It was a lovely hotel, we had good food and accommodation, and everyone was feeling very happy. On one of the evenings, I know that it was after dark, your father left me in our room at the hotel. He didn't say where he was going at the time, and he went out somewhere alone. He was gone quite a long time, and when he came back to our bedroom, I mistakenly asked him where he had been. And when I asked him this I really angered him, and he grabbed a hold of me, dragged me into our shower area, he put on the shower to drown out any noise, and he started beating me around the head.

I don't remember it, but after this happened we must have gone to bed, and the following morning when I got up, I was very badly bruised all over my face. I pleaded with your dad not to expect me to go down to breakfast and face the students, but he wouldn't listen to me. He insisted that I go down and face everyone with my face badly bruised. It was as if he wanted to show me up in

177

front of them. I expect that at the time the students were rather shocked at what they saw, but no-one said anything to me about it, either then, or later. So after this happened we stayed there until the end of the holiday, and then we returned home to carry on with the rest of our lives.

On our arrival back home things continued as they had been before, the doctor who was attending me for my pregnancy, was the college doctor, and neither he nor the nurse who was a friend of mine, said anything to me about the bruising on my body.

After this time, you might have thought that your dad would have changed things, but no he didn't, you know how stubborn he is, and so he continued his teaching and continued travelling to London once a week for his studies there. He still insisted on having the young girl come to our home, as he said that she still needed help with her homework. He continually said to me that there was nothing wrong in their friendship, and of course it was me who was in the wrong, for saying that what they were doing was wrong.

At the time all of this was happening, I did not have anyone I could talk to about it. My family were all living in Scotland, the only friends that I had were his friends, and I could not have said anything to them without upsetting your father. Your father was always in charge, and I had to just put up with what he wanted. And of course I felt very ashamed, and I was so worried about what I thought by then, as I did think that something wrong must be going on between your dad and the girl.

But neither of them seemed to care anymore about what I did or said, they were both determined to carry on with their friendship regardless of what I thought. The young girl, knowing what was happening between us, started to get very cocky about things. She, or should I say they started doing things in front of me, probably just to annoy me. Any time she came over to our home, she would sit in a certain kind of manner as if to goad me. She usually slept over in our home the evening that they were studying, and she always slept in the downstairs living room at the back of the house

Now by this time I was within a month of having our youngest daughter, I don't know how it happened, but I went into what we thought was labour, as I started having early contractions, and it seemed at the time as if the baby was on its way. Everyone rushed around, my friend the midwife came over from the college, and she started to prepare the room for a home delivery.

I had known the midwife as a friend for some years, and this made it easier for me during the pregnancy and at the delivery of the baby. She raised the bed in our bedroom with what I think were blocks of wood, this was to make it easier for the delivery of the baby. But later we found out that I was in fact having what they called a 'false labour' at that time. But because we were now ready, the midwife decided that we should leave the wood under the bed, that way we were well prepared for when I did go into labour.

It was exactly one month later, when I did actually go into labour, and it was really an awful time for both the baby and me. The baby didn't seem to be coming down where she should, as she seemed to be coming down to the one side of my body, and as a result of this, I was having exceptionally bad contractions, and this was causing distress to both of us at the time of the delivery.

My friend the midwife, knowing that I was trying to have a natural labour, told us that I needed some help to deliver our baby. The midwife tried to give me some pain relief, but my husband said that I shouldn't have this. I obviously could not cope with the pain and your dad was sent out of the room on an errand to the kitchen. While he was out of the room, my friend gave me the gas and air, as I needed this to deliver our baby safely.

A short time later I did have our third daughter, when Joy arrived the midwife had a lot of difficulty in getting her to breathe, but she kept on trying, and in the end we were all relieved when at last she finally got our baby to cry.

That day our little daughter was born, and we called her Joy!

When Joy was born she looked exactly like our daughter Ann had looked when she was born. It was like having Ann all over again, except she seemed a bit more like Grace in her temperament. From that moment, I now had three little girls to care for and look after. And to me all our other problems didn't seem too important any more, as we now had this little new and additional member of the family to look after.

So I continued supporting your dad, saying nothing to anyone and letting your father and the young girl do just what they wanted to do. And as your dad kept saying to me, there was nothing happening between them that I should be concerned about.

And as you know of course, it was all in my head!

The truth was that I was always controlled by your dad, wives should submit to their husbands. I always had to agree with your dad in everything, he had bullied me from the very beginning of our marriage, and he knew that he would get away with it.

From this time onwards however, your father did nothing to hide his interest in this young girl from me, and I was getting increasingly worried about them. He had, as I explained before, started to get violent towards me again, just like he did at the beginning of our marriage. I had always been afraid of your father, and what he would do to get his own way. But I still had a few doubts going on in my head, as the girl was still so very young at the time. She was still a young school girl, and I was sure also that your father was totally committed to our new way of life, and that meant he would not be unfaithful to me, or have a wrong relationship with a young girl.

Now just when you least expect it, we had another surprise happen to us. We were asked to make another move as the people who owned the house that we were living in were returning from abroad, and they had decided that they wanted their house back again.

I had loved living in this house, it was the nicest house that I had ever lived in, but once again we had to start packing, and organising ourselves for another move, and this was happening not too long after I had given birth to Joy.

We were re-housed by the college, and this time we moved to a place called Borehamwood. This new house was a bit further away from the college campus, as it was quite near to St. Albans. It was further for your dad to travel to the college for his work each day, and we were told at the time that this move would be a temporary one;

they hoped to find your dad a place nearer to the college for us to live in fairly soon.

So we finished our packing, it was a bit more traumatic for us this time, because of our new baby, but all things considered, we managed, and we made another move to Borehamwood.

Your grandfather (right)

Chapter 9
Suspicious but Still Uncertain

By the time that we had made this move to Borehamwood, I had almost convinced myself that your father and the young girl who was our babysitter were both having a wrong type of friendship. But they were very clever in what they did, and I could not prove anything. All that I had to go on were my own feelings and my thoughts about it. They were both doing their best to convince me that everything that they were doing was quite normal between them, but my gut feeling was telling me different! As I said before we were dealing with a very clever man, he knew me, and he knew just how far he could push me. But by this time I was almost sure that they were both lying to me.

So she kept coming over to be with us, and she even came over to this new home that we had just moved into. Her parents still seemed very happy about their friendship; and he cleverly covered up what they were doing as we were always having some other young lady college students over to visit us at home at the time. Probably this was just a smokescreen to put me off, and to help them cover up what was actually going on.

But I had no proof that I was right, I was only going by my feelings at the time. But as the weeks and months went by, it became harder and harder for them to hide it from me, and as a result of this, I became more certain that I was right as each day passed by. It even got the stage in this house, that when she came over he would order me to go up to bed early in the evening so that they could do the homework. This meant that they were alone in the living room together while they were studying. For me, it was very much like being a prisoner in my own home and I couldn't do a thing about it. I was not allowed to question whatever he did at any time. And what made it worse was that I did not have any proof, as he was always so very clever at covering things up.

One of the days when he was in London he telephoned me at home, and when we spoke I asked him again if anything was going on between them, as by this time I was quite certain that they were wrongly involved with each other, and his reply was "What should I do? Do you want me to jump under a train?" and of course I said no to him when he asked me this!

I should have known by the time that he had said this that I was right about them, but then he later denied it again, and I was left wondering, but fearing the worst! I didn't know what to do about it at the time, I was so confused about the whole thing. And I did my best to keep things as normal as I could for my little family.

As I said, we always had lots of visitors to our homes, and it was no exception in this new house that we were now living in. It would have been easy to say that I was jealous, and that I was wrong to be suspicious of what they were doing. This was always what your father

186

would say to me any time that I asked. But by this time, I was nearly certain that I was in the right about them, all I needed was the proof of it. And of course if I was right, what could I then do about it?

All I knew was that I was continuing to get increasingly concerned at their unusual behaviour, and this seemed to be only in front of me. It was as if they didn't care a bit about what I thought. As I said, everyone outside of our family thought that your dad was a devoted husband and father! But if I was right in what I thought, I knew that your dad would lose his job, and that there would also be some other very serious consequences for us to face.

The house in Borehamwood, although not nearly as nice as where we had been living before, was very adequate for our needs. We settled in there, our little family seemed to be very happy at this time. I can remember that in this house we had huge glass doors out to the garden. It was winter during the time that we were there, and I can remember leaving my children inside the house, while I tidied the garden outside. I also made the effort to clean both sides of the huge double glazed doors that we had there. Because I could see the children inside the house, I was able to keep the huge doors closed as it was freezing cold outside at the time. While I was doing this, my children were comfortable in the warmth of the inside of the house.

I didn't have any transport of my own at this time, and I can remember that a girl that we knew from the college came over one day, so that your dad could take me to do the family shopping.

Your dad continued to go to his work at the college campus each day, and he also continued to go on the journey to London University each week. He was still studying there for a doctorate, as this was to help the college with their accreditation.

By this time also, I was finding some funny things happening when the young girl was coming over to our home, but I was afraid by this time to say anything to your dad about this, I had no proof, and they continued to say I was wrong.

We knew that we were only in this house for a short time, and as this house was a little small for us as a family, I was pleased when I heard that we were moving once again.

Ann the cheerleader, at the college

Chapter 10
And at Last the Truth Came Out

You know, if anyone saw this house that we were moving to in Radlett, they would think how very lucky we were, and how very blessed we were to be going to live there as a family. We would only be renting this house through the college, but this new house that we were moving to was amazing. The house was right in the centre of Radlett, it is a lovely area to live in, and for our children to be brought up in.

The whole of the house was lovely and clean throughout, the college paint crew had done a most wonderful job when they got it ready for us. They had painted the whole of the house from top to bottom. As far as I am concerned, no-one could have asked for anything more! We had a lovely family, your dad had a good job, and we had (thanks to the college) a beautiful home to live in. We were not rich people, but I should think that anyone looking on would think that we were, and they would think how lucky and how rich our lives were.

And what is more, your dad was so highly thought of at the college, and together we as a couple had some amazing opportunities. We even got the opportunity of dining with some very important people who were visiting the college in the faculty dining room on some evenings. We also had several visits to the houses of people who I considered were much more important than we were. We were invited to many weddings, and I can even remember meeting a very well-known American man, he came over here to attend one of the weddings that they held in one of the big houses in Bricket Wood. It was truly a wonderful experience for us to be invited there that day. I think that what I am trying to say here is that your dad was treated very well by everyone, we were having a ball here at the college.

Actually I would say that for us at that time, the sky was our limit!

But you know what, all of this time, in spite of the opportunities that he had, your clever dad seemed to be both obsessed with, and controlled by a little girl who was then about fourteen years of age.

Our new home then was a well presented detached house, with its own secluded garden at the rear. It had three bedrooms, a study, and a bathroom upstairs. It also had a lovely big dining room for us to have our meals in, and in addition it had an exceptionally large lounge. The lovely hallway was the size of some rooms today, with the staircase going up from the hallway to the bedrooms upstairs. The kitchen downstairs was large and it had an adjoining utility room, and also a downstairs toilet. This house was really very special, and it had leaded lights for the windows.

I knew that I could not help but love living there!

So on one of the days that your dad had off from his work, we left our children with the Davis family and we went out and chose some lovely Axminster carpets. We chose the same carpet for the whole of the house, and a different colour of the same carpet for the dining room. Also at the same time we bought a new three-piece suite for the lounge. We bought some dining room furniture for our lovely new dining room and I remember that we also bought a really nice matching set of bookshelves for both the stereo equipment and for our very many books. All of these things were to make our little family more comfortable. I am sure that no one could have thought or even imagined that there was anything wrong at home.

Now who could ask for anything more? I certainly could not, with of course the one exception to this!

During the time that we were living there, I was trying to keep things as normal as I could. I had my three little children to look after, a lovely home to keep nice and many college functions to attend. We visited the families that we knew, and yet at the same time I was convinced by then that something was seriously wrong at home. No matter what your dad said, I was now convinced that there was something wrong going on between him and the girl, but I had no proof of this, and your father always denied it.

Things continued to be difficult at this time of my life, in spite of the fact that we had so much going for us, and I tried to cope with this on a daily basis. The housework was easy for me, I had always been a very fit person, and even with three young children to look after, I found that the house was very easy for me to manage. In this house we had all of the modern equipment that was about at the time. We had a dishwasher and a washing machine and a tumble drier, so there was really no very hard work for me to do there. I could easily take time out, and I would get my children ready each morning, and I would take them to the swing park that was at the top of the road each day. The children would really enjoy their time there, and it would give me some time to think about what was happening in our lives.

At this time your father was still progressing well in his career, and one day each week he still travelled to London for the degree course that he was doing. He would always travel there by train as the station was now very near to where we were living in this house.

Everything seemed perfect for us as a family, as I am sure any onlooker would have thought, but it would seem however that there was one person in our family who wasn't happy with what he had achieved. He needed something more, or should I say someone more than what we could give him, or perhaps I should say, that I could give him.

You almost cannot believe it, we had everything going for us, our children were lovely and healthy and happy. Your father had done so well at his job, we were managing financially, we had some really good strong friendships with other people, and we had a lovely home to live in. But unfortunately here was I still having to worry about a little girl of around fourteen years of age, as she was about that age at this time. But although I couldn't prove it, I was sure that something wrong was going on, in spite of the denials from both of them.

But your father was so clever, he was always one step ahead of me in everything that he did, and he always had an answer for everything that he was asked.

In spite of all that had happened, nothing seemed to stop your father and the girl from the friendship that they were developing. They were determined to carry on with their friendship, and they were now getting away with causing big problems within our little family. In this house that we had just moved to, we were again living quite near to her parents, but she continued to come to visit with us, and she would stay overnight at our home on the evenings that they were studying. And this meant that they were both controlling what was happening within our family.

You know that no-one could have asked for anything more than we had at this time of our lives. Everything that we had was so very good, the children were really happy and getting a bit bigger, and they were getting easier for us to manage. The Davis girl should have been happy as well, she had nice parents and a lovely home of her own to live in. She went each day to a private school that belonged to the college, and she was really one of the very privileged young people who were able to go there. As well as this, she was also having free private lessons from your father to help her at school. Shouldn't this be enough for anyone!

But what was to happen afterwards, proved to me that they were both lying to me!

So as most people would expect, we were gradually getting more settled into this house, the house looked lovely with all of the new furniture and furnishings, and the new carpets that we had bought had just been fitted in there for us. I know that at this time, we would both have thought how lovely the house looked!

So the routine that we would have had, was that your dad would go to work each day, and I would keep house and look after our children each day. When your father came home in the evening, we would all sit and have dinner, just like most other families do.

The only other thing that was badly affecting us as a family, and was now spoiling our lives, in so far as I was concerned, was this little girl who was becoming more and more like a part of our family as each week went by. She did not seem to want to go away from us, or spend some of her time with anyone else. I still wonder what her parents were thinking about at the time, they must have really preferred the time that they had to themselves. That was silly of me wasn't it? Of course they did, and I expect that this was the reason that she was always with us.

And of course your dad was happy, our little children were happy, and it seemed as though I was the only one who was having doubts about the wisdom of it. Most of the people who knew us would think that I was being very silly, this little girl was about fourteen years of age by then, and she was from a church family. Nobody could possibly have thought that anything could be wrong with their friendship.

Except me of course, as by now I had convinced myself that there was!

Our life at the college was such a good one, and a unique experience, and I loved every minute of it. You know, I was able in this situation that we were in, to be a mum who was at home all day with our children, not like mothers today as they mostly all seem to have to go out to work. So you can tell that we were managing financially at the time. But from this time on, your father did not hide his interest in the Davis girl from me, and I very reluctantly accepted this very unusual situation that we were living in. What was I to do about it? I was afraid of your father, and of what he might do if I said anything more to him, or to anyone else about it.

So as we continued with the usual routine that crops up in every family, something happened that gave me a breakthrough, and I knew then for certain that they were both lying to me. There is a saying that says, "be sure your sins will find you out", and they were no exception to this. Because as it happened, their sins did find them out in the end!

Now I know that anyone reading this will put the blame at the one person's feet, and although I am not excusing him as it was very wrong of him, some children are more advanced than others. I know that the girl was fully responsible for her actions, because I know what was happening in our home.

This young girl knew just what she was doing, she wanted your dad, and in the end she got what she wanted!

Suddenly on one of the evenings that she was with us, they slipped up, and I knew then for certain what was going on between them.

It was when we were all together for the evening, we had finished our dinner, and for a period of time after this we all played and had some fun with the children. I then took the children upstairs to bathe them all. Bath time was always great fun in our house, as our children would all get into the bath together. Joy was obviously still a baby, but she also loved the times that she was held there, playing with her sisters in the bath.

While I was with the children, your father and the babysitter settled themselves down on our nice comfortable carpets in the lounge, and they got themselves ready to do the girl's homework. After the fun of bath time was over, I dressed the children and brought them back downstairs again to say goodnight, and so that they could be cuddled before I took them back upstairs to their bedrooms.

So with all the goodnights said and everyone feeling happy, I took the children upstairs again, and I settled them down in bed for the night.

After this, I got on with my usual routine, I tidied the bathroom and then I went downstairs to clear up after dinner. I always left the washing up until after the children were safely tucked up in bed for the night, as this way, it didn't take me too long to get organised again. I went into the dining room as this was the first room that I usually did, and then I took myself into our kitchen. I loaded the dishes into the dishwasher, and I wiped all of the work surfaces, and by then I felt that I had done everything that I should.

Unlike today, I had to have everything looking spick and span. Perhaps that is what I did wrong? I was too fussy as I loved everything spotlessly clean, just like my mum had done!

Usually it took me about an hour or so to clear up after the dinner, and it was during the time that I was doing this that the Davis girl came into the kitchen and she kissed me goodnight, and she told me that she was going to bed. So I said goodnight to her and happily continued with my chores, as by this time I had almost completed my work. Then knowing that she had gone to bed, I began to think that your dad and I would have a quiet evening by ourselves listening to our lovely music.

Should I say that I thought it at the time, that we would then have a quiet evening in? I think that you can tell from this, that I still loved your dad, and I also really enjoyed the times that we would spend with each other as he was always such good company.

Anyway with all the tasks of the evening completed, I think a good song here would be, 'now is the time that I am hoping for', only thinking about it now, I should have been singing instead, 'now is the hour for me to say goodbye'... because what happened next was a complete shock even to me, in spite of the suspicions that were in my mind about the two of them!

I walked into our lounge, I was thinking that your dad would be in there and hopefully still doing some of his own studies; but much to my surprise the room was empty. Your dad always played such lovely music when he was home in the evening, and I thought that now that our little family were settled down for the night, that we would be able to enjoy this together. But where had he gone? I suppose that at the time, I must have been curious about where he had gone, as I began then to start to look for him. But I would say that I wasn't expecting what I found that evening!

Anyway I went out to see if he was in the back garden, or by the car. When I did not find him there, I checked our front garden, our kitchen, our dining room, again into our lounge and he was nowhere to be seen. Now it was at this point, that I realised that I would have to look upstairs!

Now as I said, the whole of the house including the staircase was fitted with lovely new 'Axminster' carpets. I am sure that your dad did not hear me as I started to go up the flight of stairs. But you know, my nature is to give everyone the benefit of the doubt, and I really didn't expect what happened that evening. But what did happen that evening? You may well ask! Well on the other hand, you may not, because you would have worked it out before me, and because you know what happened later! I hope that none of you my children, are as stupid as I have been in my life!

Anyway I slowly crept up the stairs, I didn't make a sound, but in fairness and benefit of the doubt, although I was trying not to make a noise, I checked all of the other rooms that were on the landing. The study, the bathroom, our bedroom, the bedroom that Grace and baby Joy were in, and they were both sound asleep. And you will realise I was left with only one other room to check that night.

Now usually in this house, our oldest daughter Ann would sleep in the same room as the Davis girl, and I was now just outside their room door. I was slightly nervous by this time, as I knew that your dad was not in any of the other rooms. I could see that the last bedroom was in darkness, but I also knew at that moment, that I had to go in there that evening!

So I slowly opened the door of the bedroom that Ann and the Davis girl were in; I walked in; even after all of this time has passed, it is still very emotional for me to tell you this. Don't forget, this is what changed our lives from then on. What I saw when I entered the room was your father lying on the Davis girl while she was in the bed.

And it was at that moment, that I realised that I was right all along!

I don't even know if Ann was asleep at the time, I probably woke her up though, because I was so very shocked to see your dad there, that I started screaming. And I knew when I saw this, that this was not just a goodnight type of kiss!

When your father heard me screaming he knew that I was in the room, he quickly jumped back off of the bed and he ran towards me. He then took me out of the room and into our bedroom. This was as you can imagine a very traumatic time, but I cannot remember any of the conversations that we had at that time, or what else happened that evening. I was probably still in shock at the time!

And it was after this happened that evening, that your father started threatening me. He told me what would happen if I told anyone!

Now that it was all out in the open, they could not deny it any more!

I continued looking after our children, and running our home. But from then on out, it was them against me all of the time. I had to live with two people who were deliberately doing whatever it was that they wanted, right in front of me and the children. My children were all very young, and of course they did not understand what was happening at the time.

I can remember that after this time, I spoke to them both together and individually, to try to knock some sense into them. I told them of the serious consequences including your dad losing his job. But they would not listen to me, and sadly they continued doing what they wanted to right in front of me. They were both determined from then on out to continue with their relationship.

Now all of this happened around spring time of that year, Joy was still a baby, Ann and Grace were both too young to understand what was happening, and at the time I realised that we could not stay there in that situation any longer.

The following day after your father had left and gone to the college, I packed clothes for the children and myself and prepared to leave for Scotland. I was just about to leave when suddenly and unexpectedly your dad came back home again. He would not let us leave, and he said that he would kill us all if I tried to leave.

Your father was a very desperate person by this time, he didn't want anyone finding out what was happening to us, and because of all of the violent episodes in my life in the past with him, I fully believed that he was capable of killing us all, and in fact I still do believe this!

So when your father said this, I took the cases upstairs again and I started unpacking!

What was I to do about this awful thing that was happening to us? It was sometime after this that he took me to our bedroom, the children must have been in bed at the time; he said to me that he could easily kill me with electricity, and that no-one would know. He had some wires in his hand at the time, and I know that he was plugged into the electricity supply. He told me to take one of the wires in my hand; and when I did this, he then asked me to take the other one, and when I reached out to do this he pulled it away from me, and he said that if I had touched it that I would have died.

You can tell that he was a very worried person by this time, and he made it clear what would happen if I told anyone what was going on in our home. At the time I believed him, he was an electrical engineer, and I thought that he would know the facts about this!

Later on, on several different occasions, he tried to use various scriptures in the Bible to try to prove to me, that what he was doing was all right and within the law of the Bible. But if this was true, and if he had believed this before, why did he not speak to me and ask me if I could accept this? If they believed this, why were they deceiving me? I don't think at all that he believed this; if he had, he would have spoken to me a lot sooner than this! He was telling me that it was all right to take another wife, just so long as she had not been with a man before, and of course, I'm being quite cynical here (and the band played.... believe it if you like).

Now from his actions after this happened, and from then on out, I felt that my life was threatened and I was constantly on my guard. I was afraid of what he might do to either our children or to me. They had now been found out, and from this time on, I had to deal with these two people who were deliberately doing what they wanted, and they did not care what I thought. And this was happening right in front of my very eyes. I was told in no uncertain terms, that I must not tell anyone what was going on. Your dad knew how afraid I was of what he would do, and he expected me to do what he wanted.

From then on, I was living in quite difficult circumstances; I was constantly on my guard. All the people in our church and the ones at the college lived in a very close knit community, and it was hard for me to pretend that things were normal in our lives.

All the way through I have said that the girl was very young at the time, I think that by now she was probably about fourteen years old, but she was not a child, she understood how to sit with her legs poised in a certain way, she deliberately wore a see through nightdress to go to bed in. I know that your father did an awful thing, but what I am saying, that as far as I am concerned, this girl was not fooled, she knew just what she wanted, and she understood how to get it. The Davis girl was very advanced for her age!

The people who were fooled were me, her parents, our church and ministry, and the college and school where they both attended. And of course our very many friends.

Your father, in spite of how he was then living, continued with his work at the college. And during these times, I was the one who was trying my best to keep things at home as normal as was possible for our children. When he was home he tried to convince me that what he was doing was biblical. He said he could take another wife as long as she was a virgin. I didn't believe him, he had certainly, apart from anything else, gone about this the wrong way, we didn't live in America, we lived in Britain (incidentally some years later, before they married under Danish law, he found out where I was working in Manchester; he telephoned me and he asked me if I would go to live in America with them). And it was at this time that he said to me, that the Davis girl was not worth the trouble that she had caused him!

However, I did do something that you would probably think was strange. I prayed about it, and I believed that if two people prayed about the same thing, that God would hear their prayer and answer it. I went up to one of the lady friends that I had known now for some years, she was from a family who were some of our closest friends from London, and I really believed that I could trust her. I told her that something really bad was happening in my life, and I said that I could not explain to her what it was. I asked her to pray about my problem, that I could have intervention for this. The lady would have realised just how serious it was from what I said. She must have thought it strange, but she didn't at any time ask me what the problem was. But I know for certain, that she would have remembered me, and what I was asking her to do for me.

There was absolutely no point in me trying to talk your father out of what he was doing, I had already tried this, and he was determined that he was right, he was always in the right, and he continued on as if there was nothing wrong with what they were doing.

It was very difficult from this time on as everywhere that we went socially, I had to pretend that we were a happy couple, and I had to pretend that your dad was devoted to his work and to our beliefs. From this time onwards I felt that I was a prisoner, and I did not know how I was ever going to get out of the situation that I was in. Don't get me wrong, I still loved your father, and I know that I would have loved it if the situation could have been reversed.

So the year progressed, and we were now heading for spring. Some people are so clever in getting what they want, and your father was no exception to this. Between the two of them, they decided that they wanted to have a holiday together. Now a family that we knew at the time had a mobile holiday vehicle, and they decided that your father would hire it, and they would go off together in it in the summer. They also decided that they would take our two oldest children with them. And of course, this was whether I liked it or not. They just had one obstacle to overcome though, and they even thought up a plan for dealing with this!

Your father was to ask the girl's parents over for a meal one Saturday evening to our home. During the time they were with us, your dad told me that I was going to ask her parents if she could accompany us on a family holiday to help us with the children. I was also told to arrange the meal for the evening.

The day of the dinner came, and as was the custom in our home, I made the dinner that evening. Her parents arrived at our home, accompanied by their daughter and their young son. The girl was obviously in on the plan to deceive her parents, and at the dinner table the conversation came up about holidays, as yes, in spite of my feelings, I did exactly what your father told me to do. Now as you now know, I was under threat at this time as I didn't know what your father would do if he didn't get what he wanted.

The parents of the girl were only too pleased about this, after all your dad was an important faculty member, and they were very pleased for their daughter to have this opportunity to be with us. At the time I was hoping that they would say no, that they were going away themselves, but they agreed to let her go, and as usual they and I went along with whatever it was that your father wanted.

After they had her parent's approval, all they had to do was arrange with the family who owned the vehicle, and wait for the days to pass by until the time of the holiday. I was not involved with any these plans of theirs. The camper van was to be their accommodation while they were away, and in order to avoid anyone getting suspicious, your father told me that they were planning to take our two oldest children with them on the holiday.

As they didn't want me around our home area while they were away, they told me that I was to take baby Joy away in the family car for a holiday. Joy was still under a year old at the time, and I think that I may still have been breast feeding her. I certainly cannot remember getting any bottles for her when we were travelling in the car. They also told me that I had to travel to the Cornwall area on holiday.

All during the time leading up to the holiday, when your father arrived home each day, he would ask me who had telephoned, why they had telephoned and what they wanted. He wanted to know if anyone had been round to the house, or if I had been out, and who I had spoken to. He was watching me at every turn, and to me it was a bit like being under house arrest. At the time that this was happening, I was afraid of what he might do next, and so I went along with him and did as I was told.

Your father, in spite of how he was now living, continued with his work at the college. He also continued travelling one day each week to London for the PhD degree that he was trying to get. I continued to try to keep things as normal as possible at home for the sake of our children.

And so we continued on, a rather tragic story, but your dad was convinced that he was right, and that I was wrong as usual, and that I was jealous of the young girl. I did what I think that most other mothers would have done under the circumstances, and I carried on secretly hoping that something would change to make things right once again. Your father was still working very hard as he usually did, while at the same time he was trying to hide what was happening from the other people that he knew.

I know that most people would be thrilled if they had what I had, because it seemed to onlookers that I had it made. And truth be told, I really couldn't have asked for anything more physically. I had a really lovely home to live in, people who loved and cared for me within the organisation that we belonged to, and yet I could not bear to be in our home any longer than I had to, and all because of the terrible things that were happening in our lives. And I didn't even know how to sort this out!

As the holiday time approached, neither of them seemed to care about what I thought any more. They were both determined to carry on with their plans, regardless of my feelings. They were obviously excited to be going away together, and when the day of the holiday arrived, I was dreading this as much as everything else that was happening to us at that time. But during the lead up to this, I continued to try my best to keep some normality for the sake of the children.

So the day came, and your father picked up the vehicle and the young girl he was going away with; they were already all packed and ready to leave for the holiday. I had been told to pack clothes for Ann and Grace to last for the time that they were going to be away, and I was told by your father that I was to go to Cornwall with Joy. He then ordered me to take Joy to the car, and it was at this moment that I broke down, and I tried to persuade them not to go. When I refused to leave, and said to him that I wasn't going, he told me once again, and when I still refused to leave your father beat me up in front of both our children and the Davis girl. He said that if I did not leave that day, that they were going to take my baby with them on their holiday as well.

Now what would you have done at that point in time? I didn't think that I had a choice. I really believed that they would have done this to me, and as usual I did exactly what I was told. I took the carry cot with Joy inside it, and I put in into the car. I also packed my cases and some baby things that I would need into the car, and I drove off.

I really have no idea where the two of them went with my two young daughters. Apparently they had been seen travelling north by someone, but I do not know anything at all about their holiday!

My daughter's Ann and Grace

Chapter 11
They Ran Away Together

As you can imagine, I was in a very distressed state when I left Radlett that day. I did exactly as I was told by your father and I headed in the direction of London as I was hoping to pick up the road to Cornwall. This was not a holiday for us, Joy was in her carry cot, she may even have sensed what I was feeling at the time, but she would not have known what was happening to us. I was both upset that my husband an apparent pillar of the community was away with the Davis girl, but I was also very upset that they had taken my two other daughters with them. And it was especially upsetting for me, that neither one of them seemed to care anything at all about what they were doing to our family.

So I left that day thinking that I had no alternative, but to do what your father had told me to do. The holiday was forced on me against my will. It was to be a holiday, whether I like it or not! Before I left that day, I was told when I had to return home again, and that I should go away with Joy. So I know that you will realise that I left home very reluctantly that day!

I travelled until I reached the outskirts of London, I have regretted since not making a note of where I was at the time I was away. But this isn't surprising, as I was very tired at the time. It was getting dark and I pulled up outside of some houses that I saw, as I thought that we would both be safer near to where people lived. I looked terrible as I had been crying and my face was badly bruised and swollen. We didn't have any accommodation for that night, and I was too embarrassed and upset to try to find us some.

I can remember the journey quite well, you probably think that this is silly, but I think that I said this to you before; I believe that we have angels who look after us at some times in our life, and I think that I met two that night! I was sitting in the car, it was very dark, and a couple came out of one of the nearby houses. They had seen my car parked in the road, and they came up to me and asked me why I was parked there. They talked to me for some time and they saw that I had my baby in the back of the car with me. These two kind people invited me into their home that night, as they said that I needed a good night's rest, so that I could continue with my journey the next day.

Many times since this happened to us, I have wished that I had the details of where they lived. I would have liked to have thanked them for being so kind to us, but alas I was in such a state that I drove off the next day after breakfast, without taking down any details of where we were at that time. Since then I have been unable to write and thank them for putting me up that night.

But baby Joy was as good as gold throughout that whole period of time; it was as if she sensed that something was wrong with me. I am not sure, but I may even have been feeding her at the time. I am certain that I was, as I cannot remember getting any bottles for her on that journey, and I do know that I was able to change her by reaching into the back of the car.

So the next day after we had breakfast, we set off once again on our journey, and because we had been so well looked after, and we were well rested, we were able to continue the next stage of our journey. I travelled quite a long way that day, and before it started to get dark I began knocking on doors and trying to find us a place to stay the night. I did this quite a number of times, but each time I knocked on a door they turned me away. Not many people were interested in putting up a bruised woman and her baby, and eventually it got too dark for me to find anywhere for us to stay the night.

I do not know where I was at the time, I was really worried that we did not have a place to rest for the night, but I also felt that I was too tired to continue driving the car, and so I decided to stop and rest for a short time in the car. I wasn't there by the roadside very long, when a police car pulled up beside me. The driver asked me where I was heading, and I told him that I was en route to Cornwall; I explained that I could not find a place to stay the night. I said to him that I had tried to get some B & B accommodation, but everywhere had been full. I also said that I could not drive any further without a rest. He asked me to follow him to a nearby car park that was in a large square somewhere near there. He told me that he would have the police patrol cars check on me periodically throughout the night, and he said that I would be safe in the car; and able to get some sleep before I continued my journey.

Early the next morning I fed and changed Joy, this was very easy to do in the car, and after we were organised once again, we headed on our way. Later that day, I started to look a little earlier for accommodation, but I continued to be unsuccessful in my efforts. I was getting really rather concerned about this when I pulled up at a garage for petrol. I was speaking to the attendant who was working on the till, by this time I was really rather anxious, and so I asked her if she knew of anywhere that I might find us a place to stay for the night. The lady (was she another angel) kindly told me that there was an empty flat above the garage, and that we could spend a few days there.

What a relief that was, at last we could have somewhere settled to recover from our ordeal. As it happened, we were able to stay there in this flat above the garage for the rest of the time that we had to be away from our home in Radlett. The lady who helped us would come upstairs from time to time and talk to me, she wanted to know what had happened as I was still bruised. I am sure that she must have been very curious about me, as I was travelling about with such a young baby.

This lady came to see me each of the days that I was there, and perhaps because I was away from home and with a stranger, I began to be able to tell her what was happening in our lives. She was really concerned about us, and she said that I should see a doctor, and when I agreed to do this, she arranged for me to visit hers. She very kindly looked after Joy while I was visiting her doctor, and I also went through the story with the doctor.

He listened and said to me that I should go to the college authorities as soon as I returned home again, and that I should tell them what was happening. I explained why I could not do this, and said that I was afraid of what your dad would do to us.

We stayed in this flat for the rest of the time that we were away, and I then said goodbye to the lady who had befriended us and started the journey home again. Again I do not remember where I was at this time, but I am sure that we must have been in Cornwall at that time. I vaguely remember being in Bath at some time in the past, and I think that I had Joy with me, it must have been then!

When we got home, everything was just as before we left, your father and the Davis girl had enjoyed their time away. Ann and Grace had also had a good time, and we were back to pretending that everything in our family was normal. I can remember the days that followed this holiday; I found it so hard to cope, as I could not say or do anything right. I tried talking to them once again, I was trying to get them to stop what they were doing. I even pointed out again what the consequences would be if they were to continue with this, and if they were found out, but I might as well have been talking to the wall. They would not listen to me, and I felt at the time, that I was living in a nightmare of which there was no way out.

Sometime after all this happened, the Davis girl had to go away on a school trip, and when she went away things settled down normally for us again, it was so strange that we just seemed like a normal family once again when she was not around. I was in dread of her returning after the school holiday, if only something could be done to stop their relationship, but alas this was not to be!

Now actually there was something that happened that changed things in part, but I didn't know about it until sometime later on. During the time that the Davis girl was away on this school trip, she wrote a letter to your father, it was sent on airmail paper to the weather satellite station at the college, where your father worked!

I found this airmail letter some months later; this was when I was asked to leave the bungalow in Bolton. Now as I said, this letter was sent on airmail paper, and it was very clear from the wording of it, that the girl thought that she may be pregnant. She quite clearly said in the letter that she was concerned because she had missed her period. It seems obvious to me later that she was, and that it must have happened during the trip that they had together in the camper van.

Then suddenly something happened and everything changed overnight, I would think that I must have been near to breaking point at the time. I had a visit from one of the ladies who had been my friend since we were in the London church, and I broke down that day in front of her!

It was one day after your father had gone to his work at the college, I had spent the time as usual organising the house and the children. My friend (her husband was also on the college faculty), came round to see me unexpectedly that day. I'm not sure how it happened exactly, perhaps it was because I had been away and I had spoken about the events that were happening to us to the lady at the garage, and I had also spoken to the doctor, but suddenly I started crying in front of my friend that day.

I know that at the time that I was very afraid, I was under strict instructions not to tell anyone. My friend could not take it in at first, this sort of thing doesn't happen here at Ambassador College, and not anyway to my husband, as everyone thought he was so nice, and such a devoted family man.

But once she realised that this was really happening, she said that she would speak to the girl's father, and another man that we both knew. I said to her that my husband had no respect for either one of these two people, and said that she would have to go higher up to get us the help that we needed.

The following day I had a call from an officer at the college, he checked that what my friend had told him was true, and when he found out that your dad checked up on me each day, he arranged for quite a number of telephone calls to come into our home that day. When your father arrived home and asked me about any telephone calls, I was able to omit the call from the official.

The following day the officer arranged to have a babysitter for our children, and I was picked up by one of the ministers in his car, and I was driven to the official's home. When I got there, they discussed with me everything that was happening in our home. The gentleman who picked me up in his car that day was appalled at how frightened I was. I was so afraid that anyone would see me in the car and tell your father, that I had ducked and hid myself under the front seat of the car in which I was being driven.

We learned soon afterwards when it started to come out, that people had seen them both kissing each other when he dropped her off at her school. These people were also fooled, as they thought that their kiss was harmless. They thought that the kiss was just an innocent kiss, and because of that no-one was even slightly suspicious, it seemed that everyone thought that your father was very devoted to his family.

The following day, both the girl, and your father were taken individually into meetings at the college. The college officials had to find out for themselves what was really happening!

After the meetings, your father was dismissed from his position at the college, and also at the same time he was dis-fellowshipped from the church that we both belonged to. You may think that this was very harsh, but we are talking here of a member of the college faculty, and an under-consent-age girl.

How were they expected to decide about this?

And I know that it was at this time, that your father was warned not to lay another finger on me!

The following day we had two officers from the college came to our home, at that time your father was offered college funds to help us relocate to another area. I really can't remember now what your father thought about this. At the time they asked me if I would continue to keep our family together, and I said that this was what I wanted to do.

We could have had this help as a family to relocate, but your father and the girl had very different ideas from the rest of us. They had both been forbidden to see each other after this came out, the girl was taken to school each day and collected again by her parents. People did what they could to stop them from seeing each other, as I understood it at the time, her parents kept very tight reins on her, and when she was home, she spent a lot of time in her bedroom.

Your father seemed at the time this happened to be very upset, I remember that he cried for three days after this happened, but someone said it was not remorse that he felt, but that he was sorry that he had been found out. At the time everyone tried to stop them from seeing each other, but in fact they were secretly planning to run away together. I found this out from your father; they were passing notes to each other in the evenings after dark using a stick to reach her bedroom window. He told me that she had said to him that she was going to run away from home, and he said that he felt responsible for her, and that he had decided to go with her.

I did not know when this was going to happen, your father said that I was stronger than she was, and that I would manage on my own. I regret now not letting someone know what they were planning, but somehow I did not expect that it would happen as quickly as it did!

And much to my surprise and everyone else's shock, a few days later they were both gone!

The Davis girl (our babysitter) was only fourteen and a half years old at the time!

I am not excusing your dad, he was ultimately responsible for what happened, but I am certain that the girl knew exactly what she was doing all the way through. No-one knew where they had gone to, and at the time they just seemed to vanish into thin air.

219

Because we were at a religious college, the college obviously did not want any bad publicity in that area at the time. I will never understand though, why her parents did nothing by way of publicity, or even by any other means to try to find their own fourteen-and a half year old daughter, and bring her back home again.

Learning to dance in Bricket Wood

Chapter 12
He Took My Children from Me

I know that at the time that this happened, someone reported it to the press and as if it wasn't enough, the press started coming round to where we lived and started asking me questions. I would not get into any kind of conversation with any of them, and there was little publicity in the area at the time. But as a result of this, it was thought that I should leave the area straight away, so that the press would stop pestering me!

All we had to do at the time that this was happening to us was to find someone who would be able to put both me and our three children up, as we suddenly needed somewhere temporary to live.

Two of our church families offered to have us. And I was asked which of the two families I would like to go to, and I chose the family where I had a long friendship with the woman of the family. The family that I decided to go to at the time lived in Knutsford in Cheshire, and so we packed up a few clothes and we were driven to Knutsford in one of the college cars the following day.

In the days that followed this, some of the college students arrived at our home in Radlett. They emptied our home of all of our possessions, all of our belongings were then taken and stored in the college press building until we had somewhere else to take them to.

Suddenly our lives changed quite drastically from this point on. We had just lost your father, our home, our car, and all of our possessions, and also most of the clothes that we had. The only help that we had was from the college, and the very kind people who had taken us in. Your father had taken all of the money from the family bank account, and he had left us with only £23 in the bank. He left us with only our friends in the church and the college to help us.

Our friends in Knutsford very kindly welcomed us into their home, they fed us, and they gave us shelter for approximately three months during the time that we stayed there with them.

During the time that we were there in Knutsford, it was again time for another of our annual conventions. It was now the autumn, and most of our clothes were at the college press building. I can remember my friend taking us to the shops in Knutsford, they had decided to buy warm hats and gloves for our children, so that they would be warm enough while we were away at the convention.

When it was time to leave for this activity, we were picked up from our friends' home where we were now staying. We were driven to the convention by a college student that year. He collected us from our friends' house and he took us to the festival, and he also drove us back from there that year. While we were there at the festival, we stayed in a chalet next to the family that we were now living with in Knutsford. They provided us with everything that we needed to be comfortable while we were there at the convention.

It was very difficult, but we did our best to enjoy the time that we had there. We were attending the convention, and it was meant to be a happy time for everyone, but for our family it was quite different that year!

Everyone we met while we were at the festival were so nice and helpful to us, and after the festival was over, we returned to Knutsford where we had to spend some time recovering from the events of the past few months. After this, we had to decide the best thing to do for the future.

I had several visits from various people at my friends' house from this time on!

Firstly, I had visits from church officials; they offered us the funds that we would need to help us in the future. Our church was going to take on the responsibility of looking after all of us because your father had gone away. I also had detectives come from where we had lived in Radlett, they came and told me that they had done everything that they could, but that they had not managed to find any trace of either the babysitter or your father. We knew that they had left the country, but no one knew where they had gone.

I loved the time that I spent there with my friends in Knutsford, the lady we were living with really loved our children, and she loved having us there with them. She was so good to all of us during the time that we were there with them. She was just like a sister would have been to me in the circumstances that I was in. Being there in her home made me feel free again, and I was able to talk out all that had happened with her husband, as he was a minister in our church.

The children and I all enjoyed being there with this family, they had one little girl of their own at the time, their daughter was just a few years older than Ann, my oldest daughter. All of the children loved playing together while we adults did the normal things like shopping, cleaning, ironing and any other household chores that had to be done. During the time that we were there, they took all of us to the place where our church fellowship was being held in the Warrington area at the time, and while we were there we started to get to know the people there. Some of these people became very good friends to me later.

Our church made provision in their system for widows and orphans, and they supported their people in times like these. And from this time onwards we were given whatever it was that we needed as a family. This was because your father had left us, we were homeless, and he had taken all of the money that we had, with the exception of the £23 that he left in the family bank account.

It was because of this that our church stepped in to fill this breach for us!

As I said, we were really happy staying in my friends' home, but we could not stay there indefinitely. It was now several months since your dad had left us, and it didn't look as if he was returning. And it was then that we made the decision that we needed a home of our own again. They thought that it would be a mistake for me to go back to live in the Bricket Wood area again, because at the time the press in the local area were still trying to find out what had happened to us. And there were also other people there who were blaming me, as they did not know what had really happened to our family. I can understand the girl's family not wanting us to return to the area, as it was a very emotional time for all of us.

You could say that the decision about where we lived at that time was made for us, as I had begun to make friends in the Warrington church, and at the time everyone thought that we should look for a suitable accommodation somewhere in that area. So with the decision made, some of our new friends started looking around in their local areas for somewhere for us to live.

There was one family in our church, they became really good friends of mine later on; they managed to find a nice detached bungalow for us to live in. It was only a short distance from where they lived themselves, and as it turned out for us, we could not have found anyone better to help us at this time. This couple managed with the help from the college, to secure the bungalow for us to live in. All we had to do from then on was to wait until our furniture and our belongings were brought up to us from the college press building, and then we could move straight in there.

And this was the reason that we ended up living in Bolton in Lancashire, the same area that your father had moved away from some years before, when he had worked at a Technical College fairly near there. He decided at that time that he did not like living in this area, and he organised it so that we moved again to the south of England. But you know, everything had changed for us, and both I myself and our family had to be happy to accept the help that we were given from everyone who was so kind to us!

The bungalow that we moved to was very pleasant, it was in a nice quiet street, and it wasn't long before we started to settle in there.

Our new friends who found the bungalow for us became very good friends to me, and they would always arrive there each week on a Saturday, and they would take us in their car to church, as we did not have any transport of our own at that time.

During all the time that we lived there in this bungalow, our church paid the rent for us. I did not have to worry at any time, about how we were going to manage financially. They also organised for me to speak to someone who was involved in welfare, and the reason for this was so that I could get as much help as possible for our little family. In actual fact we were really well taken care of at this time!

The couple who found this new home for us became very good friends, and they continued helping me from this time onwards, and they were the first people who came to the bungalow to help me, just after your dad arrived and stole you from me.

So we got ourselves settled in there, the bungalow was detached, and it was really nice inside as it was very clean and nicely decorated. It had a small but nice garden and it was of course very suitable for our little family. It was while I was in this house that I later found the letter that the Davis girl had sent to your dad at the weather satellite station at the college. Sometime after they married in Denmark, he approached the church about returning to it, but because they had this letter, they knew that he was still lying about what had happened.

We slowly began to come to terms with our new life in Bolton. We had such a lot of fun when we lived there, as we continued to have a lot of contact with the family who had put us up when we left Radlett. And we also made lots of other new friends in the Warrington area, when we went to meet the people who met there on Saturdays. It was always such fun going there, everyone was so kind to our little family, and we would go to any events that they had there. We didn't have a car, and we were transported about all of the time by our friends who lived near us, and who had found the bungalow for us.

In fact, I suddenly remembered just how kind this couple were to me, they continued to come over and help me after I had lost my daughters. They were always there for me, as they took me everywhere they were going. I remember that on one occasion they were going to Glasgow for a meeting that was being held there, and they took me there with them that day.

Warrington became our local church area, and we travelled backwards and forwards there each week, as we were taken by the family, who had helped us find the bungalow.

This family who now lived nearest to us, and who had found the bungalow for us, they had young children of their own to look after. And all of the children loved meeting up and playing together. They did everything that they could possibly do to help us, during that time when we were still coming to terms with losing your dad.

So after a time things started to work out quite well for us, the friends who had found us the bungalow came over to see us fairly regularly. They would bring their big black Afghan Hound over at this time, and we all had a lot of fun with her. This couple and their children all loved animals, they had previously had a pet shop, and they loved their big black Afghan Hound. So the conversation started about the possibility of me getting us a dog as a pet for our children, and I thought that this was a really good idea.

From this time on, we all started to plan for my children to have a dog of their own; the most important thing was to find a breed of dog that we felt would be safe with our children, as they were all very young at the time. We spent the time looking through some books and studying about the various dog breeds, and we came up with two that would fit into this category.

Joy was only about a year old at the time, and we had to make sure that she would be safe with any animal that I was going to buy. At the time we could not get our first choice of dog, and our second choice that we knew that was good with children was an Irish Setter. I made all of the arrangements that were required, and I purchased our first dog. I called our dog Petra, and anytime that we all met up together, we had their children, my three daughters and two dogs with us. You can just imagine the fun that all the children had when the two dogs chased each other around the garden at our home.

My children grew to really love Petra our first dog, and we all enjoyed the times that we took her out for a walk, we had some really nice times with her.

We were really settling into our new home in Bolton; and into our life without your dad. It was his choice, and at the time that this happened to us, he had made it in favour of the young girl who was our babysitter. In spite of the things that had happened to us, we were having some exciting times there at the bungalow. Each week our friends would pick us up, and they would take us with them to our church in Warrington. We began to spend some time with the people there, and we gradually began to make some more new friends.

One of the times that we were there at Warrington, they were having a social event in the evening. It was on this occasion that my youngest daughter Joy nearly had a serious accident!

I can remember this social really well, they were having organised activities for the children in the middle of the hall floor. All of us adults were standing there watching as the children enjoyed their activities. Just at that moment Joy my youngest daughter decided that she was going to run away from the group of other children. She was so very quick on her feet after she had started to walk; and suddenly without any warning at all she very quickly ran away from the other children; and she was heading for the hall doorway. I was watching my children from the other side of the room and when I saw her run away, I chased after her and had still not reached her by the time that she had gone through the doorway to the outside of the building. By now she was running on the kerb and heading for the main road. I realised that I could not catch her before she ran into the road. I saw this huge lorry hurtling towards us and I shouted 'no' to her, and at that moment when she heard my voice she stopped in her tracks. And I realised then just how easy it would have been to have lost her!

Where was her dad at this time? Certainly not around to help me look after our little family!

Now it was around this time, that our oldest daughter Ann who was now five years old had to start going to school. She had known a lot of the pupils who had attended Imperial School (the college school) and she had been really looking forward to going there. She was really disappointed that she could not go there, but I managed to get her into a primary school that was only a short walk away from our home, and she soon settled in there, and she started making little friends of her own while she was there.

During this period of time, we all took a trip to Scotland to see my mum and my family. While we there your grandmother took you out and bought you all new coats, hats and gloves. Winter was coming on, and you didn't have any warm coats to wear. These were the ones that you were wearing when your dad took you away from me!

While we were in Scotland, we also went to visit your father's sister and her husband and their little son that they had had by then. They were so very pleased to see us, and as usual they made us all feel very welcome there with them. In fact, your aunt and uncle offered to find us a rented property there in Scotland, so that we could go to live nearer to them.

But we didn't really get time to think very much about this, it would have been nice for us to have lived nearer to our relatives! But as it turned out, it was very soon after this that your father arrived at our home and took you away from me!

I was taking advice from a solicitor at this time, as I had been advised to see a solicitor when I went to live in Bolton. I was told that I should apply to get legal custody

232

of our children. As I understood it, until the court has awarded one of the parent's custody, both parents have an equal right to have the children. And so I was advised to get custody as soon as possible!

At that time, none of us, not even my solicitor realised what was just around the corner!

No-one at the time who knew anything about what had happened to us expected that your father would return, especially not so soon after he had run away with his lover, our babysitter and his best friend's daughter!

Not even the solicitor realised just how urgent it was, and I had unfortunately left it in his hands to do this for me. In fact, as I found out later, this could and should have been done overnight at the courts, if I had but known this at the time!

Because your dad had been so violent to me in the past, and because he had also recently threatened our lives, someone advised me to have a hidden telephone somewhere in the house that we were living in. This was to be a safety precaution, in the event of your dad turning up there unexpectedly. I had the telephone installed and hidden in the bathroom in a laundry box. This was at a time before we all had mobile phones, and nobody was intended to know where this telephone was hidden.

I think that by now you will understand why this was done!

But unknown to me, your father was always one step ahead of me, he is so very clever, he had become friendly with the landlord of the bungalow. I understood the landlord was told that I had run off with his children, and the landlord told him about the hidden telephone. I would think that the landlord was probably in the house when we were out, otherwise how did your dad know that the telephone was there when he arrived there that day?

You may wonder why I would need to be protected; apart from the threats to our lives when we were in Radlett, your father had always forced whatever his will was on me, and if he found it necessary, he would even use brute force to get and achieve what he wanted. No matter how small, whatever he wanted he forced on me.

Some of the things in the earlier part of our marriage were weird to me, I had grown up as a middle child in a family, I did not expect to get my own way all of the time, but for some reason your father always did!

Can you imagine having a relationship with this man? He was very good company, and people really liked him. He could be such good fun at times. He was also very responsible in most of the things that really mattered. He was a good provider in a modest way, but on the other hand he had to have his own way in everything, no matter how very small it was.

If he objected to any action of mine, or if I objected to any of his, he would lie in bed and say that he was going to die. I have even seen him holding a sharp bread knife in his hand and start to run towards a wall in a kitchen, this was so that I would give in to him, and go along with whatever it was that he wanted. It may not have been much, but for him, I had to agree with him or else!

I was always afraid of your dad, he was so very unpredictable, and I think that I had this fear of him, from the first time that he hit me, soon after we were married and in that bedsit that we rented in Glasgow. I have tried to explain this fear of him, I don't understand it now, how

234

can I have been so afraid of someone? But at that time of my life, I was terrified of what he may do to us. I really believed that he was capable of doing what he had threatened, when we lived in Radlett!

As I said before, we were all beginning to get settled into our new surroundings, Ann had started at her first school, and she was happy there. Both Grace and Joy were happy and settled, and I was pleased that things were sorting out for us.

When suddenly there was a knock on the door of the bungalow that we were living in!

This was about four months or so after the day that he left us, when he had run away with his fourteen-and a half year old lover!

I was obviously not expecting to see him there on that day, and in fact there was no one who knew what happened to us (apart from the people who helped him of course), who would have thought that he would turn up there on the doorstep at that time.

So you can imagine what a shock and surprise it was when I opened the door, and saw your father standing there as bold as brass on the doorstep. You would have thought that it was his home, he walked right in to our new home that was provided by our church, he gave the children a hug, and of course the children were really pleased to see their father.

I was in deep shock when I opened the door and saw him standing there, this visitor was not welcome, and with good reason. So far as I knew he did not know where we lived, we were only taken there because he had left us. But to say that I was afraid of him was a bit of an understatement. He could, and he had been very violent in the past, he had also threatened to kill us all when we lived in our last home in Radlett. I could not know to what lengths he was likely to go to get his own way. I was deeply shocked when I saw him standing there, and I do not know how he could have found where we were living, without the help from others.

It was not that we were in hiding, but we hadn't long moved into the bungalow from the home of the family who had taken us in when your dad had deserted us - the kind family who had given us food and shelter after your dad had left us homeless after he had run away with the girl who was his lover; the one whom he was obsessed in his relationship with for a very long period of time.

As a result of his actions while he was teaching there, he had been dismissed from the college where he had started as a student, and where he later became part of the teaching staff. He was also asked to leave the church that had been a large part of our lives together for quite a number of years. You may think that this was rather harsh treatment of someone, but he was living a lie; I was being badly ill-treated and the girl in question was under the age of consent; the college had no alternative but to take this course of action.

When he arrived there that day, your father told me that he wanted to take you all for a four-week holiday, and as usual, I wasn't to have a say in this!

And of course as you all know from what happened later, your dad told yet another lie to me at that time, isn't seventeen years or what could have been a lifetime rather a long holiday for anyone to take?

As I said before, and in some ways I hate to say this, (because he is your father) but your father is a compulsive liar, and this is just another proof of this!

All of the time that your father was in the house he watched me, and he followed me everywhere. If I went into the kitchen he followed me there, when I went into the bathroom he forcefully insisted on accompanying me there (and he knew about the hidden telephone that I had in the bathroom). During the time he was there, when I went out to the garage hoping that I could call for help, he came out there with me until I returned inside the house again.

Your father would not let me out of his sight for a moment while he was there!

He told our children that he was taking them for a four-week holiday, and he said that he was leaving the next day. You all know that this was just another of his lies. He had no intention of taking you for a holiday.

It seems to me that he just wanted to blot me, and all of the past, out of your lives!

But when he said that day that he was taking you on holiday with him, my daughter Ann who was just over five years old at the time, said to him that she wanted to stay with me, and he turned to her and he said to her, that that was the very reason that he was taking her away with him.

Ann won't remember this, but at the time she wanted to be with me, and not with her father. Isn't it interesting? He knew that the children wanted to be with me, but to him, it was only "what he wanted", that mattered to him.

But as always their father had to have just what he wanted at any time, he was always obsessed with getting

237

his own way, he warned me of what would happen if I told anyone of what he had done. He wouldn't have any thoughts about what was the best thing for either the children or me. You know now that what he wanted was me out of the picture, he wanted to look like the doting father, unfortunately for me, some other people that he knew also thought that what he did was the right thing!

I know that there is no way that your father could have driven a car with three young children in it, including a one-year old baby, and have safely driven it away from the area where we were living, without having the help of others. He had kept me up all of the night before he left, neither of us had any sleep that night, he would not have been fit enough to do this. The police were out there looking for them a short time after he left. I do not think that a pregnant girl of fourteen and a half would have been the only one helping him. Your father was a brilliant manipulator, and he must have had people organised to help him.

Perhaps by now you will have worked out who it was who would have helped your father that day, and from then on. He must have had help that day when he took you away, and for a period of time afterwards, and until he felt that it was safe to leave the country again. I would think that they are people who you still know.

I think that at the time that it happened, both the police and I thought that you had all left the country on that day, but after giving this considerable thought and with the realisation that he must have had help; I now think that you must have stayed in someone else's home until your father felt that it was safe to leave the country

238

again. I obviously do not know the facts, but this seems the most likely explanation to me now.

At the time that your father took you away from me, Ann my oldest daughter was just over five years old, Grace was about three and a half and Joy was a baby of one-year old.

While he was there, I tried my best to keep things as normal for my children as I possibly could, I was obviously in a terrible state of mind, not knowing what was likely to happen, and all of the time fearing the worst!

I was obviously terrified of what your dad might do, as I could not predict the outcome of his time there. He kept me up all during that night sitting on the settee, he accompanied me any time that I went into the bathroom, and in fact he accompanied me everywhere. I could not get out of the house or even use the telephone, as he was watching me every minute of the time.

The following morning he left the bungalow, he said again that he was taking you for a four-week holiday and that I must not inform the police.

I know now that I should have stopped him in some way, I don't know what the outcome would have been, you hear of such terrible things that people will do if they are angered, but I do not know why I allowed him to scare me so much that he got away with you that day. Somehow I think that I did not believe that he would get away, the police were called immediately, and they did everything that they could to try to track your dad down, but in spite of all of their efforts, your father succeeded in getting away.

I can only think now that your dad had someone who was waiting nearby and willing to help him. Otherwise how did he manage to get you all away from there by himself, it just doesn't make any sense does it? The police were convinced that your dad could not have done this all by himself.

The police also alerted other police forces, and they were watching air and sea terminals to try to find your dad, but they could not find any trace of him anywhere. They said that he must have had help from other people, and or even a private boat to help him get you out of the country.

There was no publicity at all over what happened to us as a family, even when the Davis girl ran away with your dad. The girl's own family did nothing at all to get their daughter back!

Suddenly as you can imagine my whole world collapsed about me, I did not know which way to turn after this, because it was on that day that he snatched you all away from me!

After this happened, I had many visits from people who tried to comfort me and help me, by talking it over with me, but how could anyone really help me? I had just lost my family. I waited at home for months hoping that he would bring you all back, but as time was to tell, your dad is nothing but a liar. He had no intention of bringing you back to me!

As the detective said and as I realised, there were obviously other people who were also involved in the kidnap that day of my three children. I do have my suspicions about who this was, but this book is not to name names, but to tell the facts about what actually happened at the time.

But I am sure by the reaction that I have had since I met you all again, that you were told all sorts of lies about me. I hoped that in meeting up with me again, that you would realise that I did love you all, and wanted you to be with me!

But it was after this time then, that I had to face the reality of my life without my three lovely daughters to look after and care for. This was a huge change for me after six years of being a mum, and it was a huge change for my little children. My children had to live their most informative years being looked after by young girl who was nearly fifteen years old, and still a child herself.

Someone told me in the past, that your father is a compulsive liar, he is so convincing!

And without my children my life did change forever!

And it has not been the same for me since then!

He took my three daughters from me

Chapter 13
How My Life Changed

The months before your dad took you away from me, I had a custody order and a divorce petition pending in the Bolton courts, but at the time that you were taken, I was still at that time waiting for my solicitor to process the custody order through the courts. I now understand that this can be done overnight. I know that my solicitor slipped up with this, but the solicitor could not possibly have guessed how urgent this was, as no-one expected your dad to turn up at that time.

But after this my solicitors tried in vain to process the petition through the courts, but nothing could be done about this, because we did not know at any time where your father was living. We didn't even know which country he was living in, and we needed an address before we could serve any papers on him. Under British law at the time, nothing could be done unless you could serve the papers on the other person.

All of these proceedings would have been paid for by the state legal system, as your dad had left me with no means of support at the time. But as I said, we could not do anything to progress this. I would think that the divorce petition is still sitting in the Bolton courts, as it has never gone through the British court legal system.

I am trying to remember just how long it was before we knew where you were. I think that the first and only address that we had was three years later, when your father gave a poste restante address to my solicitor, from his Danish solicitor. This was when he had decided that he was going to marry the babysitter. It did not however stop him from finding out where I was at any given time. I will tell you later of a conversation that he had with me when he asked me to go to America with them, he always knew where to find me!

But you must be wondering what I did after this happened, and how I was coping emotionally after your father took you away from me. I was obviously finding it difficult to cope with my life after this happened to me. I know that I could not have done this to anyone, and somehow I could not have imagined that anyone would do this to me!

Wherever I was at any time, whether it was on a bus or train or anywhere, if I let myself think about you all I would start to cry. I was missing you all so very much! I was tempted to think that it would be easier for me to end my life, but I believed at the time and I still do, that this is a wrong thing to do. I remember standing by a river bridge on one occasion, and the thoughts came into my head at the time of how much easier things would be if I did jump in, and I pushed the thoughts aside as I knew that doing that was not the answer!

And it was when this happened to me that I realised that I must live this or die!

It was around this time that I also remembered, that my children all had a special protection (a bit like a church blessing) placed on them just after they were born, and somewhere deep within me, I believed that if I did what I believed was right, that one day I would meet you all again.

All of my friends were rallying around, they spent their time talking to me, and trying their best to help me to cope. It was during this time, that I was given a card from a Christian lady that I knew, the card was about the bends that we go through in our lives. The words on the card, and of course the help that I had from the other people that I knew, kept me going. I have kept the card that Flo sent to me, and ever since this happened to me, when I have another major thing happen in my life, I take out the card and read the lovely message that she sent to me. The card contains the lovely poem by the famous poet Helen Steiner Rice and it is called "The End Of The Road Is But A Bend In The Road".

Every time I read the lovely words that she wrote, I get the encouragement that I need to face yet another challenge. Her words are extremely encouraging and also very inspirational, and the lovely poem that she wrote, ends by saying "Your work is not finished and ended, you've just come to a bend in the road."

As I said many of my friends tried their best to help me, but how could anyone help me in this situation that I was facing? How could I even want to live without my lovely little daughters to look after?

I don't know if I told you this before but the family who put us up in Knutsford told me that they put anything that they couldn't deal with as a family, in a little box on the shelf to be taken down and looked at later. They would leave the problem there on this shelf until they were able to take it down again and deal with it. I did this to the best of my ability with my feelings, because everywhere I went at this time, I was looking at every little blonde curly haired girl, and I was thinking that she may be Ann, only to be disappointed yet again. I had to try my best to control my feelings for you all, as it was too painful for me to cope otherwise.

Because I was so distressed when I was out in public, I mentally did my utmost to stop myself thinking about you, and I tried to stop feeling any emotional feelings towards you, as otherwise I could not cope with my life!

I continued living in the bungalow in Bolton, where we had all lived together before that day when your father took you away from me. I waited there hoping that one day your father would bring you back to me. I hoped that it really was only a holiday that he had taken you for, as this was what he said, but he didn't bring you back again.

During the time that I was still living in the bungalow, the church continued to pay the rent for me, and they helped to support me. Then one day when everyone including me realised that your dad wasn't going to bring you back, it was suggested to me that perhaps I should try to find some work to do, so that I could try to support myself again.

So this was when I first started to look for work. I searched in the Bolton area, and the surrounding area, but it was very depressed there at that time, and I could not find any work there. I soon realised that if I was to get any work at all, that I would have to travel each day into the nearest city and that city was Manchester.

248

So I started travelling daily into the city of Manchester, it took an hour each way to travel by bus. I was hoping that by doing this, that I may find some suitable work that I could do. I had several interviews, and eventually I got a position working for a firm of chartered accountants who were based right in the centre of Manchester. I hadn't worked in an office since before I had given birth to Ann, but I knew that I had to make the effort, as I had to begin to pay my way once again.

The position that I got that day was as a cashier for Touche Ross chartered accountants. The first day when I arrived there for work, another member of staff who had been there for a number of years decided that she wanted the job that I was employed for, but as it turned out, I was then employed as her assistant. I did not mind this at all, because at least I was working again and for a really nice company.

So it was then that I started travelling each day between Bolton and Manchester. Touche Ross really was a nice company to work for, and I loved the work that I did for them. I made quite a number of friends during the time that I worked there, and some of us got together once a week to play badminton.

I was still travelling backward and forwards between Bolton and Manchester when sometime around then, I started having problems with my landlord. I truly believe that your father put him up to this, he would come round in the evenings and he started to harass me. He wasn't coming for the rent money, as this was paid for by the college. It was hard to find a good reason for his visits, and when I showed that I was not interested in his advances, it was kind of obvious to me that I would then be asked to leave the bungalow.

I was right about this, as it wasn't long after this that I was asked to leave the bungalow. And it was during this time then, when I had to clear out our belongings from the bungalow, that I found the letter that the Davis girl sent to your father at the Weather Satellite Station at the college. Obviously all of the clothes were prepared as they had to go to charity, and this was when I found this letter.

When your father left our home in Radlett, he had only taken a small suitcase with him, and all of his clothes were packed along with our other belongings by the students, and when they later arrived in Bolton, they had been put straight into the loft. I obviously had to go through these things though before they went to charity, and it was during this time that I found the letter in his best suit jacket pocket. It was obvious on reading this letter that the Davis girl thought that she was pregnant during the time that she was on her school trip.

So I kept the letter, everything that I did not need went to charity. I knew that all of my belongings from the bungalow were to be put back into storage at that time. I had suddenly once again become homeless. But you know, by the time that this had happened to me, I had already made some good friends in the church that I was attending. Several of them rallied around to help me, and they started looking around for somewhere that I could to go to live.

It was then all of a sudden that one of them found me a furnished flat to rent, this accommodation was near to the station in Heaton Moor, which is not far from

Stockport. The apartment was vacant, and I did get this, and I was able to travel from then onwards to work by train. It was also very near to some of our church members, and I was able to help a family who had young children while I stayed there.

So when I got this apartment, and I felt happy with where I was going to live, I finished packing up all of the items that I knew were going into storage before I left the bungalow.

I was now in possession of the letter that the Davis girl sent to your dad, and this was very significant, it was an airmail letter, and it had arrived at the Weather Satellite Station at the college that your dad was in charge of. Unfortunately for your dad, when he went off with her, he must have forgotten about it, as I am sure that I was not meant to see it.

I cannot remember all of the contents of the letter, but I do remember what it was about, the Davis girl said in the letter, that she was very worried as she had just missed her period. I think that you will know what that meant, you are intelligent young ladies, and you can work out her age, and also the age when your first brother was born. And something I have just realised, if anyone doubted what I was saying, the letter was proof of what was happening at that time. You know it is only now when I am writing this book that I have realised this.

Anyway what did happen to that letter that was in your father's best suit pocket. Well, at the time, I only kept a copy of this letter, I took the original letter to a meeting that I had at the college some years after this. I was told that your dad had asked if he could start attending our church again, but because of the letter that I had given them, they knew that he was lying once again, and he was not allowed to be in our fellowship at that time. I suppose that it must have been hard for him, when he could not get back into church attendance. But he hadn't lived with what he had done, as he was having fun at the time. I wonder when it was, that the hard reality of what they had done hit him?

I know that your father would not have meant for me to see this letter, but it was obviously forgotten about it when they ran away together. The school trip was after the holiday that they had away together, and it made me realise that she must have been pregnant when she left the country, and this was later confirmed when I went over to Copenhagen for the divorce. They said there in the courtroom that she had a young child, who was about three years old at the time of the court hearing.

Now when I moved into my flat in Heaton Moor, I started to be much more settled as a person. It was very pleasant living there as it was quite a compact little apartment, and it was very easy for me to manage. After losing my family, it seemed to me that I had lost my whole world, and this little place was ideal for me. I didn't need a big place to live in by myself. I was able to walk from the flat-let to the train station each day, as I caught the train to go to my place of work. I still had the first job that I had found in the Centre of Manchester, and I had also met some of the people who lived near me and who attended the same church as me, so I made many friends while I was there.

After a time though, it became quite a burden for me to keep paying the rent in Heaton Moor, and also the monthly storage bill for my furniture, I was really struggling, and I had to once again ask the church to help me. I realised then that I would have to start looking for an unfurnished place to move to, so that I could reduce my monthly outgoings.

So this was when I started to look for my next home!

I went along one day to the nearby Stockport Council offices, and I asked them if they could help me, but they could not help me at that time. I think that I have said before that I believe that sometimes angels help us, and that same day, just when I was leaving the council offices, I was approached by a lady that I hadn't met before. I thought at the time that I had met another angel. She walked right up to me just as I was leaving there, and she handed me the name of someone who worked in a housing association, as she thought that she would be able help me.

So armed with the name of this lady, I went to where the lady worked and I spoke to her. I explained to her about the predicament that I was in at the time, and she said that she would help me as soon as she could. I know that you may think that I am weird, but I was sure then that I believed that had met another angel!

Anyway it wasn't long after this that I received a telephone call, and I was given a really nice two bed-roomed flat to live in, I was then able to remove my goods from storage, and have all of my own belongings around me once again.

So I did all of the organising that was necessary, and planned my route and travelling arrangements to get to my place of work each day, as I was from then on travelling to work from a different part of Manchester. I was still working for Touche Ross chartered accountants at this time.

It was sad though, that even although I had moved out of the bungalow, I was still being harassed at my work by the landlord who owned it. He had been given my work telephone number by someone, I wonder who that could have been? He started harassing me once again, he telephoned me on several occasions over his property, and he said that I had taken (I think that it was an axe) from his garage when I left there. But I knew that I didn't take it, but because I had lived there, and because I wanted to stop him calling me at work, I paid him the money for a new one so that he could replace it. I then told him that if he contacted me again at any time, that I would inform the police. I heard nothing more from him from that day onwards.

Sometime soon after this, I had a telephone call from your father, he knew my work number! Your father always knew where I was, and I will always believe that your father was the one who was using the landlord to stir up trouble for me, both at my place of work, and when I was at the bungalow.

During all of this time, I had solicitors trying to locate your father, but they could not find any trace of him. We couldn't serve any papers on him at any time, either over the custody order, or so that we could process a divorce through the courts.

Very shortly after this I had a telephone call from your dad at my work number, as I mentioned previously, your father always knew how to find me. He said that he was in Manchester and he asked me if I would meet him. I can remember that I met him after work one day, we did obviously talk, but I cannot remember anything about the conversations that we had, or even the reason for his trip to Manchester.

There was another time that he came to Manchester, it was during the time that I was still living there, but I know that it was at different time. I think that it must have been three years later, when he had decided to marry the Davis girl. I can remember that I agreed to see him, but because I was worried about him coming at the time, as you know I was always afraid of what he might do, I asked a friend that I had in the church to be there with me for the meeting.

He came to my flat that day as arranged, it was then that he told me of his plans to marry the Davis girl. This was after he had previously said to me that she was not worth the trouble that she had caused him. I think that the main reason that he was there that day, was so that I would start to sort the divorce proceedings out. He wanted to get a divorce in Denmark and under Danish law, and this could only be done with the full co-operation of my lawyers here in England.

And it was on that day, that he left me a few photographs (how kind) of my children!

Isn't it strange how people behave? He made sure that I did not know how we could contact him, but as soon as he wanted something, there he was sitting in my home. He made no apologies for what he had done to me in ruining my life, and in taking my family from me, (he still hasn't, and neither has she) but here he was, asking me to co-operate with him as he wanted to get a divorce to marry the girl.

Talk about insult to injury, this is something to really think about!

Here was my husband, I could hardly believe it, I still can't sometimes, he had deliberately stopped my solicitors processing any of the paperwork that they required, he snatched my children away from me against my will, and now he wanted my co-operation, because he wanted to get married in Denmark to the girl who helped him rob me of my children. Because as it turned out, in order for them to marry under Danish law, he had to be divorced from me.

All I can say is that he is selfish to the end!

Anyway it was after this visit from your father that the legal things really did start all over again. I told my solicitor about his visit and his intentions. As you know I had applied to the British courts for a divorce and a custody order for my daughters, but my solicitor could not serve any papers on your father because we did not know where he was living; we had reached a blank on this. Now that your father wanted a divorce it all had to be sorted out!

It's strange actually how when you are faced with things, without thinking of the motivation behind it, you go along with it. I know that they later had a second son, perhaps this was why they were going to get married at that time. I will never know the answer to this.

Anyway, I think that you all know the outcome of your father's visit to me that day, yes as always he got just what he wanted! We did all of the paperwork that was necessary in order for him to get his divorce in Denmark. This was all done under Danish Law, and with the full co-operation of my solicitors here in Britain.

After this visit I contacted my solicitors with all the latest developments, and I was told that although the divorce and custody would be conducted in the Danish courts in the Danish language, that they would give me a Danish lawyer to represent me on the day. I was told in advance that I should go over there for the court hearing. I was also told that I would not be allowed to bring my children back home again, the reason for this was that by this time my children had lived in Denmark for over three years, and that after the hearing in the court, that they would be made wards of the Danish courts.

So armed with this advice from my lawyers in Britain; I did once again what I was told to do; I travelled over to Copenhagen to meet the lawyer who was acting for me, and attended the hearing in the court.

I found it very difficult that day in the court room, I did not understand any of the proceedings as they were all in Danish, but I did my best when something was translated for me to put my point of view. But the end result of this was not what I really hoped for, because I truly believed that children should be with their mother. Not with the father, and especially one who had run away with an underage girl. But on that day, and because you were all settled at school over there, the judge would not let you return to England with me, and you were all made wards of the Danish Court. I had been told that this was what the outcome would be before I went over there, but deep in my heart, I could not believe that this could possibly happen!

Incidentally it was said in the court that the Davis girl who was with your father that day was entered in the court as his domestic help and not his future wife. They did not mention her age, or the fact that she already had a son by him, or that she had gone to Denmark carrying his child.

The young Davis girl, (who later became your stepmother) and your father came up to me just after the court hearing, they asked me if I would like to see you before I left for home. This took me completely by surprise, and I said <u>no</u> to them. I think that I was shocked at their approach and also I was taken aback that they could both approach me in that way. It was not that I didn't want to see you, but that I knew that I could not bear to see you, and then walk away again. I could not bear to go through all of the trauma and the pain of the past few years all over again. I feel certain now that this was the wrong decision to make, and I have to live with that, but I thought that it was the right decision at the time. I was very surprised at their approach to me and I was still shocked at the judge's decision, knowing that I would have to come back home to England without you!

So sadly I arrived back home in Manchester, your father and I were now divorced under Danish law, and all of you, our children, were made wards of the Danish courts. Your dad was now able to marry the Davis girl in Denmark, but the decree that he got there was not recognised under British law. Unless the law has changed, I would think that when they later returned to Britain, that they were not considered to be married under British law.

I had done all that I could legally do at the time to bring you back home again, but your father had won, yet again he was clever, and he got himself a divorce and he was able then to marry the Davis girl. Also at the time that this happened, he also got the custody of you all!

Now at the time that this happened, Britain was not a part of Europe, and there wasn't a Court of Human Rights in Europe that I could appeal to, and I realised that day that I would have to face the future without you.

Now I do not know where your father worked at that time, but I do know that he must have been earning a good wage, as in the court, knowing that he would have to finance looking after you, the Judge of the Court ordered your dad to pay me around £200 a month for two years from that day. But I only ever received one payment of this into my bank account.

Your dad, clever as always did a nice little trick with this. The first payment arrived at my bank and in my name, as you know my Christian name is an M., the rest of my name was your father's surname, so I was Mrs. M etc. Your father initials were C.M. and his surname. The first payment that was to be paid to me through the Danish court system arrived. The second payment that arrived at the bank was paid into an account for C.M. and our surname. Your father organised it so that the money was being paid into an account for himself and not to me.

He is so clever, and he could always out-smart me, and of course everyone else he comes into contact with!

After I returned to England, I assumed that your father had married the Davis girl, the girl who was our baby sitter and his best friend's daughter. I didn't hear anything from them or about them after this, not until the day that I met the kind gentleman from Bricket Wood some years later.

I also found out on my return that the Danish decree that I now had was not recognised here in Britain, at the time I was not concerned about this, as I believed at the time that even with the Danish decree, I could not marry again. So I accepted this as I still considered myself to be married to your father during this period of my life.

So after the journey to Denmark, I carried on with my life and with my work for Touche Ross. I don't know how long I worked there for this company, but it was certainly more than three years. As everything was decided legally now, I knew that there was nothing more that I could do, but try to carry on with my work and with my life.

So I did this and got on with all of the many events in my life, but all of the time, in my head, I still wanted to go back to where I had lived with your father. I wanted to again go live near to the college, where your father and I were based before your father left us. So after what I thought was a reasonable period of time, I asked the college officials if as far as they were concerned, I could go back to live in the college area again. This was where I had spent the most of my adult life, and where I believed that most of my closest friends lived. The reason I asked, was because of what had happened to our family; I knew that some people may not want this.

I was so happy when I was told that yes, they could not think of any reason why I could not do this. I obviously should have worked out all of the details first, but I am fairly impetuous as a person, and I made the big mistake of handing in my notice at my place of work, and I also notified the housing association as they also needed notice from me before I left my flat.

So without thinking any more about it, I started my packing and getting myself organised, when I suddenly received a message asking me not to go back there as some of the people who lived there said that they would not be happy if I went back there to live. So here I was, once again I was being blocked from doing what I really wanted to do; surely this wasn't such a big deal; but the advice that I was given was not to go there!

Now if I fast forward to where I am now, I would not go back there to live, I have found an inner happiness and contentment where I am now. Yes, I think that I have really moved on as a person, as I don't think anyone wants to be where they are not wanted, and I certainly do not!

Anyway after being told that I should not go there, I immediately went back to my employer to see if I could reverse my decision to leave there, but unfortunately they had already replaced me at work, and the home that I had been living in had also been taken by someone else. So here I was, yet again I was homeless and I did not have a job. I obviously had no alternative but to find another home and a new job once again.

The housing association who owned my Stretford flat in Manchester, were thankfully very sympathetic to me because of what had happened, and they very quickly found me another flat to move to. I made this move and once again was happy to be given somewhere that I could take my furniture and my belongings to.

The next thing on my list of course, was to find some kind of work to do, as I still had to support myself. So once again I was out there doing my job search. I had several interviews but as you know, it is never easy to find work. I had not had any special training at that time of my life, and jobs were very hard to find. Another problem that I have is that am always very nervous at interviews. I still am today, and I was told that this always shows up when I am being interviewed by anyone.

One day when I was in the job centre near to where I was living, and because I could not find any office work at the time, I started considering doing something completely different. I began thinking that I would like to go into either nursing or some other kind of caring profession. The career lady at the job centre said that she thought that a nursing or a caring profession would not be suitable for me at that specific time because of what I had been through. She said that she thought that I had been through too much trauma in my life to do this kind of work. At the time she knew that I had worked in an accounts environment, and she suggested to me that I take up some kind of training for this.

Up until this time, I had called myself a book-keeper, but I had not received any formal training to do this. The career officer who knew this suggested to me that I go to a college and receive this training. She asked me if I would be interested in attending a course that had just started at the time, at the Altrincham Business College in Cheshire. She said that she knew the principal of the college, and said that she may be able to get me on the course.

And of course I jumped at the chance of this training. The next thing that happened was that she spoke to the principal of the college on my behalf, and the principal agreed to interview me, even although the term time had already started. So I went to meet her, had the interview with her, and she very kindly agreed to allow me to take the course that she was running. So from then on, I became a student of the Altrincham Business College in Cheshire.

The course I took with the college was a six-month full time course, and if I qualified and passed the exams, I would then become a qualified book-keeper and a qualified typist.

I think that I met many angels at that time of my life!

Most of the students at the college were studying to be top secretaries, and they were learning both typing, shorthand, and O level English. The course that I did, was all of the typing to the advanced level, and the 'O' level English. But the main part of the course that I studied for there was "The Principles of Accounts", and if I passed this, I would then have a qualification as a book-keeper.

It was the autumn when I started this course, and the principal of the college taught everything there apart from the typing, she had only one other lady working for her, and she taught all of the typing to the advanced level.

This was a fairly intensive course that I was on, and at the time that I did this, it was like having private tuition, as there was only one other lady doing "The Principles of Accounts" when I was there. We both had individual and personal tuition from the principal of the college.

I loved the time that I was there at this college, I spent some time getting to know some of the other ladies who were there, and I really enjoyed my studies. The college principal was fairly strict with all of us who were there, she was quite old school in her approach to her

263

training, but her college had a good reputation locally for turning out good people, and I know that she wanted this reputation to continue.

I have always been very grateful for the training that I received there at the college. I know that what I learned there helped me for the rest of my life, as it gave me the confidence that I needed to go out there and to do a good job for any employer that I worked for. I thought that the college principal was such a caring person, she treated us all so well, and I felt really blessed to be on a course there, and also so pleased to get to know her!

So here I was, at the end of my course, and ready for the next lot of interviews. I could now go forward, knowing that I was fully qualified, and that I was more than capable of doing a really good job for some company out there. At the college I passed "The Principles of Accounts", and also I had the added bonus of having taken and passed all of the Pitman's typewriting examinations up to the advanced level.

I said my goodbyes to both my typing teacher and the college principal, I was really sorry to be leaving there at the time. I was told by the principal of the college, that she thought that my ideal job would be to work at one of the big London hotels as a receptionist book-keeper. She thought that this would be my ideal type of job!

Anyway at the time, I was living in Manchester, and all I wanted to do was to get a job in my local area, so that I could support myself again.

So here I was, only this time I could be much more confident when I went for interviews. I did have several interviews at the time, but I did not have any success. It was then that I spotted an advert in the newspaper for a position working as a cashier for a firm of chartered accountants, and they were based right in the centre of Manchester near to where I had worked before. At the time they were looking for a cashier to work in their accounts section. I can remember the day that I rang the number, the lady that I spoke to said that they had received over a hundred applications, and that they had already narrowed it down, and that they were about to offer the position to one of the people that they had already interviewed.

I told this lady that I was speaking to, that I was very interested in the position that they were advertising, and I asked her if they would consider keeping it open, and giving me an interview for the job. And much to my surprise, the answer that came back was yes, all I had to do then was go through their interviewing process.

I went there, and I had the first interview with a really nice man who was an accountant, he was one of the partners of the company at the time. I knew later that he was not the senior partner, as I did work for the senior partner later when I got the job. Anyway the interview seemed to go well for me, and I was asked to return for another interview later, and this was with a different gentleman who was even higher up in the company.

I had this second interview, and it went fairly well for me that day. It was not very long after this that I received a letter from the company, and they offered me the position working as their cashier.

You can imagine how excited I was at this time, the job that I now had, was for a company of chartered accountants called Tansley Witt. This company later became part of the Arthur Andersen Group, and as I understand it, they became independent from Arthur Andersen again later. I do not know if they are still in existence today. I had a lovely job working for this company, as at the time they needed someone to do their clients' salaries, their own dispersments, their own ledgers, and various other accounting responsibilities.

And of course, I now had the confidence to go and work there, and with both my qualifications, and my hard work ethic, I did really well when I was working for them. At the time, I also made some good friends with the people who worked there. I stayed working for them for a number of years after this, and until my life changed once again, and I was then on the move and heading for Birmingham.

While I was in Birmingham, I did manage to get a position working for a chartered patent agency in the centre of Birmingham, this was before they had the euro currency. I did all of the foreign ledger work for them. They were dealing with countries all over the world, and this made the ledger work really interesting for me. While I was there, I also did all of their banking, and various other accounts duties for them. All of the work I did there was manual as we didn't have computers at that time!

While I was in the Birmingham area, I also worked for a company in Birmingham who made various articles of ladies clothing, and while I was there I did their payroll and their reception work for them.

I had another sudden change in my life, and I ended up back in Manchester. When this happened I lived in a furnished room, in the upstairs part of a house owned by the family of a church friend of mine. This house was in the Salford area of Manchester. I got on really well when

I stayed there. The lady of the house was such a friendly and lovely person, another one of the nice ladies that I have met during my lifetime. She had this lovely big dog, and I really had some fun with her dog. After I came home from work in the evenings, she would come upstairs to the apartment that I was living in, and she would sit and watch me, and keep me company. It was lovely and fun when she was there as any time that I started to sing, she would join me and sing as well! I did have such a nice time living there in that house! While I lived there I did accounts for a company who imported lady's shoes.

I again spent some time in the north part of Birmingham, and because things were constantly changing for me at this time, I went to live in Earlswood overlooking the lake. I was near to Henley in Arden when I lived in Earlswood, and I would often go down there for a coffee to one of the coffee shops. And it wasn't long after this, that I took my first trip to the famous town of Stratford-Upon-Avon.

During a period of six years I worked for The Birmingham Hearing Centre, I was dealing with both their private and National Health patients. I did all of their accounting and some of the reception work for them. Because I worked there and did their banking, I was able to obtain a mortgage to buy my first flat in Stratford.

So this was yet another move for me, and it wasn't long before I settled into my new flat in Stratford-Upon-Avon. I loved living in Stratford and from there I could travel by train to my work in Birmingham.

I continued working for the Birmingham Hearing Centre as their Accounts Manager, until a member of their family decided that she wanted to take over my position, and I ended up leaving the company at that time.

Anyway with my job as accounts manager gone, I started to work in both Redditch and in Stratford as I had just bought my first flat. I loved this little flat that I had in Stratford, it was only a short walk from the town centre, and the river. I started to do a lot of walking at this time, and I decided to buy myself another dog. I bought myself a lovely little King Charles Spaniel dog, and we both spent many happy times walking around the Stratford and the surrounding areas. To me Stratford is a bit like Edinburgh, always a lot of people walking about and enjoying themselves, a very buzzy place!

During all of the time that I was moving around it was my practice to continue attending the church that I had belonged to. One day when I was living in Stratford, and going weekly to the Birmingham church, a man that I had known from years before who knew that I loved to sing, suggested that I travel to the Northampton area and join the choir there. He suggested to me that it would only take about the same time to travel to Northampton for our services.

And this was indeed a good idea for me at the time!

I was once told that I looked a bit like a gypsy, I have moved so many times that I think that I should have been one!

Our meeting after seventeen years

Chapter 14
We Met Again Seventeen Years Later

From then I began attending the Northampton church and I gradually made a lot of friends in that area. It was really nice for me because I was able to be in the small choir that they had there in our church at that time. And as you know, one of my favourite things is singing. I was also very pleased to be going there, as I began meeting once again with some of the people that I had known from years before when we attended the college.

So with my mind now in another gear, I started the journey from Stratford to Northampton each week. And after a time, I started taking part in very many of their after church activities, and it was then that someone said to me, "Why are you travelling all of that way each week? It just doesn't make any sense; would it not be better if you lived a bit nearer to your friends?"

After this discussion, and after thinking about it, I decided to try to sell my house in Stratford. At the time we were in the middle of another recession, and it was difficult to sell houses even in Stratford. I gave this to an agent and because they could not sell it for me, I withdrew it and several months later I advertised it in the local newspaper and I sold it privately to an Australian couple who were moving to live in Stratford.

During the time that my house sale was going through, I was looking for property in either Northampton or in the Milton Keynes area, and that was when I saw and bought the house in Milton Keynes that you all came to when you visited me soon after we had met up again. It was a lovely little semi-detached house; just a minute's walk away from the canal; and only a short walk away from the very nice 'Willen' lake.

When I arrived there, it was still during the recession, and it took me quite some time to find a permanent job to do in that area. I did an extensive job search along with a number of other people from the employment offices, and after a time I managed to secure a nice accounts job in the area. By this time of my life I was fairly settled as a person, my little house that I was living in was nice after I had done it up, and I was having a very acceptable time there as a person. The house was a very pretty little house (my first renovation project), it had a good sized rear garden and in fact was really a perfect place for me to live. I lived in this house for quite a number of years (doesn't time pass quickly?) and I was really very happy there.

By this time, I also had a good many friends living both in Northampton and in Milton Keynes, and I could easily travel by car to meet up with them whenever I wanted. Life became really good for me as a person in this house, and I began to settle down more as a person while I was living there.

Somehow living in an area and near to people that I knew was almost like being back at college for me. I enjoyed spending a lot of my time with many other people whom I felt that I could trust, it was so nice being near my friends again. I really loved my time there, and it also helped me as a person to be able to be a part of a choir once again, because as you know, I love singing!

It seemed to me at that time that the only problem that I had, and that I would continue to have in my life, was that my little family were missing, and I did not even know where you were. You were all still in that little box in my head. I couldn't let myself feel any emotion for any of you, but you were always there in the background of my mind. I believed at this time, that you were still living somewhere around the Copenhagen area, and the only address that my solicitor had for you was the post restante address that we had used when your dad wanted his divorce.

But this move that I had made to Milton Keynes was probably the best one for me, I was once again living fairly near to many of our church families, and being near to them was a big help to me as a person. I knew that my life would never be the same without you, but I had learned to adjust over the years, and I soon settled down yet again, into this new area.

There was always though an emptiness in my life, but I had accepted that I may never see you all again. This was always a great sadness to me, but one that I had been forced to live with!

Gradually though, my life became more bearable for me as a person, my church friends helped me to put a second hand kitchen in the house, and once I had painted the house and tidied the garden, the house looked very pretty, and it was always a pleasure to go back there.

And this was the house that you came to just after we met up again!

It was during the time that I was living in Milton Keynes and attending the church in Northampton that I started to get involved in visiting the homes of the many friends that I was now meeting. And because I had friends living nearby, I was able to start entertaining my own friends. As I said, life was really good for me at that time!

It was also during this time, that I got the opportunity to travel with my new friends; we went to some of the social events that were held in our various churches around the area. We all enjoyed meeting up with other people, and several of us would travel to the different areas together. On one of these occasions, we heard that they were having a very large social at Ambassador College in Bricket Wood. And you can imagine how I felt when I heard this. I had been asked not to go back to live there, but no-one had said that I could not go back for a church activity with a group of my friends.

Ambassador College was the college that your father had attended as a student, and where he had later taught on the faculty. It was also the place where he had formed the relationship with your step-mother, and it was this relationship that had caused him to lose his job there. It also was the reason that he left our home in Radlett to run away with the girl who was his best friend's daughter. Some months later he came and snatched you away from me, when we were living in Bolton.

But I was really excited about this; all of my friends had decided to go for that occasion. You can imagine what this meant to me, surely no-one would object if I attended a social function there?

The day finally arrived and I was especially excited. And yet at the same time I was still feeling rather nervous and apprehensive, not that I had anything to worry about. I knew that I would meet some of my old friends again, but just going back there after all of this time was quite traumatic for me!

Little did I know at the time, what was about to happen that day!

Anyway we all travelled on our way, I think that on this day we were travelling between Northampton and Bricket Wood. It was quite a long way for us to go there for one evening's activities. But we were all feeling enthusiastic at the time, and it didn't seem to matter to us how far we were travelling. We were all used to attending our various church functions, and we were used to having to travel wherever they were held. It was always so good for us to be with people who thought similarly to us about so many different issues, and we knew that we would have a great time fellowshipping with some of our old friends while we were there.

The social evening was being held in the college gymnasium, and it must have been attended by a few hundred people. I know that we would all have rushed around when we arrived there, as we were all trying to catch up with the people that we had known in the past, as it was always exciting to meet up with our friends. Many of these people we probably would not have seen for some years, and it was always good to find out how people were getting on in their lives.

I am sure that they would have provided a buffet for all of us to enjoy at the time, and also they would have had some activities that we could all join in. I was especially pleased to be there; I hadn't been there since we had left the area years before, and it was good to be able to be right there on the college campus after so many years away. Remember I had spent some of the most informative years of my life there, and because I loved being there, it was almost as if nothing had gone on in between. I was back once again in the place that I loved!

But what was about to happen next, was a really big surprise to me that evening!

I remember that I was sitting alone at the time, and I was watching other people enjoying themselves, when a gentleman who was a former friend and colleague of your father's came up to me. He was on the faculty when your father taught there, and I knew that they knew each other fairly well. And this is the man, who was responsible for changing my life yet again. As I said, this gentleman was one of the college faculty, and he was teaching there when your dad ran away from the area with our babysitter.

I didn't know this man very well myself when I was at the college, but he came over to me and he asked me how I was keeping. We spent quite a bit of time talking, if you remember I hadn't been there for years, and an awful lot had happened during this time. And it was during the course of the conversation that I had with him, that he asked me if I had seen any of my children, and of course I said no. I still thought that you were all living somewhere in Copenhagen, which in those days was like the other end of the world to me.

The man said to me that I was mistaken in thinking that you lived in Copenhagen, he said that you had all returned to Britain several years before. Now you can imagine just what a surprise this was to me that night. You were all back here, but not one of all of the people who I knew had told me that you were living somewhere in Britain. And this was several years later. I could hardly take it in!

Now I am getting very emotional here, just writing about this. It still brings tears to my eyes!

I was obviously delighted to hear this news, but in a way, I was also shocked. How was it possible that your father had returned to this country, and that he had continued to keep you my children away from me?

Neither he nor the Davis girl who he was now married to had done anything at all to reunite us. They would both have known how to find out where I was living. It would have been easy for them to trace me through the church that I belonged to. How can people be so cruel? It was not as if I would have run away with you! Did I not have some rights as a mum, and didn't my children have the right to know me if they wanted to? I knew that my children were older now, but they could at least have had the opportunity to meet their mother if they wanted to!

You know, I am not surprised any more, at man's inhumanity to man!

Anyway I continued talking to this man, and if he reads this I would like to thank him, because he was the one who changed my life again. I will never be able to thank him enough for telling me about this. It wasn't that he shouldn't tell me, but no-one else did, and many other people a lot closer to me would have known about this. There would have been many people including the girl's family who knew where they were!

Was everyone who knew him afraid of your dad?

Anyway as it happened, the gentleman could not tell me where you were. I did ask him and he did not know where you were. I asked him if he could help me with any other information, and all he knew was the name of a couple that your dad regularly associated with. And I knew that these people were close friends of the Davis family.

I knew that the girl had lost her mum sometime after they ran away together, but I would have thought that both her father and the other members of her family would have known where she was living. I know that this would not have been a big secret from them!

Now I feel sure that I would have said thank you to this gentleman, I have not seen him since the day that he told me this. So I would like to thank him once again for the help that he gave me that day. If it was not for the things that he told me, I may not have met my girls again!

I knew that your aunt (not a real aunt) would have known your whereabouts, but I had not seen her for years and I know that she wouldn't have helped me to find you anyway. Some years before this, she had come up to me at a festival and had upset me by bragging about her trip to Copenhagen. She told me what a wonderful time that she had had with you all on a trip out there, and this had really upset me at the time!

Now what I found interesting was that when we did meet up, you told me that you had been looking for me. Could none of your family have told you how to find me?

It wasn't difficult to find me through the church that I still attended.

Why was it that everyone wanted to protect your father from me? I don't understand it; he was the violent one, not me!

But at least I now had some information to at least help me to find you. I knew the name of the couple who were in touch with your father. Now this couple that I am referring to were both very elderly at this time, and no-one would have wanted to upset them, I certainly did not want to! But if they were seeing you as a family, then they should be willing to give me some information to help me find you. I know that they would not have been the ones who helped your father take you away, but they may even have put you up there with them. I think that the day your father took you away, he would probably have stayed at least overnight with someone.

Anyway by the time I am writing this book, I know that they are both deceased, and so nothing I say can harm them in any way. Your dad was always very good at covering his tracks, but now that I had this bit of information to go on, perhaps at last I may be able to be in touch with you again. I decided at that time that I would try to think of a way to approach this couple, to try to find out where you were living.

If you were ever in any doubt about your father's desire for me to be involved at any time in your lives, you will know by now that this would have been the last thing that he would have wanted. But why? I had been a good wife and mother, why did he not want me to spend any time with you, what could he possibly have to hide?

I had been told sometime in the past by a minister in our church, that your father had asked if he could attend the church again, you may remember that he had been dis-fellowshipped because he had the affair with the Davis girl. I was told that he went to a meeting to ask the church about this, but when he went to the meeting he lied yet again about their relationship. The church officials knew this, because they already had the letter that I had found in his jacket pocket on their file.

Anyway my thoughts at this time were that I should get in touch with this couple; as I said they were really very elderly by now, and I must try to not do anything at all that would upset them. I knew who they were, they had not been close friends of ours, but they were very close friends of the Davis family when we were all at the college. So I knew that I would have to tread very carefully, so as not to upset them in any way.

But when I left that evening, I could almost not take in what I had just heard, and yet I was also very excited at the same time. I knew then that evening that one day I would meet up with you all again, and that was thrilling news to my ears. I also realised that your father was obviously not going to unite us all, he was not going to give me a chance to meet up with you again. But why not? This was years later, and I was your mum!

I had however been given some information, and I was certain this might lead me to where you were!

And it was on that very evening that I resolved to do my best to try to find you all!

There's a song that comes to mind here that I used to sing in the days of my youth. The words are quite fitting, to my mind anyway:

'I'll see you again, whenever spring breaks through again,

Time may lie heavy between, but what has been is past forgetting

These sweet memories, across the years will come to me

Though my world may go array, in my heart will ever lie

Just the echo of a sigh, Goodbye!'

Now if this goodbye was not forever, I now had my opportunity to try my best to find you and change it, at least in some measure. But because of the things that had happened in the past, I realised that I must tread very carefully, as so many other people's lives had been involved with what happened to our family.

So after considering how I should approach this; and because I did not want to upset this elderly couple who knew your whereabouts; I decided that my local minister may be the person who could approach them on my behalf; and ask them where you were living. So I spoke to him and he said that he was very happy to do this for me.

After a week or two had gone by, he came back to me and he said that he had spoken to the couple, but unfortunately they said that although they knew, they were not prepared to get involved. So I had now come to a dead end over this. But while I was speaking to the minister, I asked him what I should do, and he said to me, they are your children, and you are entitled to do what you want to find them. I thanked him for trying to help me, but I knew at the time that I was no further forward than that evening at the social in Bricket Wood.

I am afraid that I cannot understand this couple, I had already been deprived by this time of your childhood, and I was your mum. And my children were not babies any more; they were now young people by this time. Yet these people would not give me any information at all that would help me find you.

It was then that I knew that I would have to do this search by myself, without any help from others.

It is not the purpose of this book to name names, the people who helped your dad over the years, they know who they are, and they were unfortunately taken in by someone very clever and very devious!

It was your father who told me that he did not want us to have any children, I was the one between us who wanted a family. I was the one who fed and nurtured you, and looked after and cared for you, when your father was pre-occupied with the little Davis girl that he was obsessed with. And this was quite some time before our last baby Joy was born.

I wonder if you have worked it out yet, what age she was at the time that this was happening in our lives. You probably know her age better than I do, you grew up thinking that she was your mum, so you probably do know her age. I know that sometime after we met up again, she left your father. The last thing I heard was that she had re-married and that she is living in Spain with a new husband. And your father later re-married himself, and surprise, surprise, he went to live in the cold north of England that he didn't like!

Isn't it interesting that they were so desperate to be together, that they had run away and ruined our family, but even at that, their own marriage did not last as they broke up sometime after we all met up.

It does not matter to me what excuses or reasons they may give for what they did, your father was in the wrong. They were both actually in the wrong, although we excuse her because of her age at the time. It must be obvious to him now in his new life, and with a new wife, that he must think of the past, and the words that he said to me when he telephoned me in Manchester that day. He said that the Davis girl was not worth "the trouble that she had caused him."

You know you can fool a lot of people a lot of the time, but you cannot fool God!

The truth will come out!

There is something about us human beings, we follow a leader and we take sides, sometimes we do not know that what the leader is saying is true or not, but because we like them, we might even think that they are important, we go along with what they want anyway.

I still cry occasionally, in my lonely moments, when I think of all that I have lost, yes, lost. I choke, just because he didn't want me to have any happiness with my children, he took them all away from me. Remember what he said to Ann when she was just five years old. She said to him "But daddy, I want to stay with my mummy", and he turned to her and said "and that is the reason that I am taking you away."

Up until this time, your father has been much too clever for me, how can you deal with someone who seems to have people around him who are prepared to back him up, no matter what he may do? But you know, occasionally someone comes along who gives you a break, or unknowingly gives you something to make you have some hope. You get the encouragement that you need to keep on trying, and to help you to deal with your life.

And that is what happened to me that day on my visit to Bricket Wood!

At the time that I decided to do my search for you, there wasn't a television program called 'Long Lost Families' that I could ask to help me with my search. But something that had stuck in my mind from my childhood, was that the Salvation Army had managed to trace some people (I think that it was perhaps after the war) as they tried to bring some families who were lost back together again. I decided at this time that I would approach them and see if they would be able to help me. I suppose that I should have considered that it would cost me a fee, but I just thought that this service was done purely to help people. I had a fairly low paying job, and a mortgage, I didn't have any available money to pay for this kind of service. So once I heard that I would have to pay a fee, I knew that I could not afford this, and I abandoned this as an idea!

I had my daughter's birth certificates, and I tried various government departments and they said that they would not be able to help me.

And from this time on, I knew that it was down to me to find my family on my own!

I know that looking back on it now, that I should have done this a lot quicker. But Britain is a big country, and I didn't have a lot to go on. Looking for someone in Britain when you don't have a clue where to start looking, is a bit like looking for a needle in a haystack. I also didn't have a lot of time, as I worked full time to support myself, and I also had a home to run.

At the time I could not think of anyone else who could help me. And while I was thinking about it, a thought came into my mind, if the Salvation Army could do it, why couldn't I do it myself? So with this in mind, and with my thinking cap on, I continued to think about this, and I wondered how I could tackle it.

As I had already tried to find my daughters using their birth certificates, and I had come up with nothing, I continued to think about how to tackle it. When suddenly the thought came into my head, what if I gave up on the idea of trying to find my daughters, and I started to look for their father instead? So with this thought continuing to go through my mind, I couldn't think of anything else that would be better for me to do at the time.

I knew that the surname was quite a common one, but I wouldn't have thought that there would be many men, even in Britain, with that surname and with the same initials as your dad. All I had to do was search the length and breadth of the country including Scotland to try to find him.

Now where could I start to do this? And of course I thought of the reference library, and there actually was no-where better for me to be at this time, than living in Milton Keynes. They had a really good reference library there, and it was right there on my doorstep. I was at the time working in a full-time job, and it was hard managing to find time when the library was open, and I didn't have work or something else to do. But I decided then that this was what I was going to do!

The first time that I went to the library, I asked one of the assistants who worked there where I could find out some information that would help me. And it was then that I could have given up, as she seemed to think that I had a crazy idea in my head, and that I was a bit strange. But I was really determined to do my best to trace my daughters, and so I continued to hope that there was some way to do this.

So regardless of her reaction, I spent my time initially going through council records, this took me some time, there are a lot of records out there to go through. But each time that I looked through these records, even although I knew the name of your father, I still kept coming up with a blank; perhaps he had not registered with a council?

So after very many visits and spending a lot of my time doing this, I abandoned this as an idea. I knew that I had to think of another way to do this. I was getting near to the point of giving up altogether, but there was always this little thing going on in my head, and it was telling me to keep trying. I knew that something else would come into my mind, and that it would help me find the information that I needed.

So sometime later, the thought came into my head, that if your dad lived in Britain he must have a telephone in his home. But where do you find someone who is good at covering his tracks, surely he wouldn't be listed in a telephone directory? He could possibly be ex-directory, and I wouldn't be able to find him anyway.

I thought even before I began this search, that I would not find him anywhere; he could even be listed under the Davis girl name. So in spite of the realisation that I might not find the number anywhere, I decided to start my search of all of the telephone numbers in Britain. But you know what, surprise, surprise, this was where he slipped up!

So I began again, my visits to the library became more frequent, I had a lot of ground to cover, and I began to think of where he could be living. I thought perhaps Scotland or even the southern part of England, I didn't think that he would want to live in the cold, damp north of England as I knew that he would not like it there.

I won't say it; you know the name that I was searching for; I continued my search and I could not find any trace of your father, but I was not going to be put off easily. I was prepared to do the work, it was not easy, but I knew that I had to continue doing this if I were to ever find you. It was a long and laborious search for me, and it took very many visits to the library. I expected that your father would be more likely to live somewhere in the southern part of England, and so that was where I started my search.

So I continued on with my search with the limited time that I had to spend in the library. Little by little, day after day, month after month, I think that it must have been years later, when I had my first breakthrough!

I found a telephone number, I don't know now which area that it was in, but the person who was listed had your father's surname and the same initials that he had, so you can imagine how excited I was when I found this.

I went home that day, and of course I telephoned and spoke to the person who answered the telephone. It turned out that it was the man's wife that I was speaking to at the time. After explaining the reason for my call, I asked her if I could speak to her husband. As soon as I

287

had spoken to him, I realised that I had the wrong number as the person spoke with a different accent to your father. The name in this case was just a coincidence, as I knew then that it was not your father. But instead of putting me off, this was the encouragement that I needed to make me try even harder. I knew then that if I could find one number with the same initials as your father, that I would be able to find another one.

So I continued with my search with any spare time that I had. I would go to the library and I tried to systematically cover all of the different areas around the south of England, as this was where I thought it would be that your dad would be living. After having a near success, I had to keep on trying!

And much to my surprise and delight it happened once again. I had found myself yet another telephone number of a man with the same initials and surname as your father. You can imagine what it felt like when I came across this. Was this the one, or would I find out yet again that it was the wrong number?

So clutching this new number I returned home that day. I was going out that evening to Northampton to a special leaving party for a friend. Within a few days he was leaving to go to live permanently in South Africa. We were all sorry to see him go, and we decided that we would have a special evening for him, so that we could all wish him well for the future.

I knew that I was going out that evening, the friend who was taking me to the party knocked my door to ask me when I would be ready to leave. I asked if he would come in and wait until I had called the new telephone number that I had just found on my visit to the library.

Most of my friends knew that I was searching for my children, and so he wasn't surprised when I asked him to wait with me at that time!

Anyway, you can imagine just how I felt, at that moment in time my heart was racing. I knew that I had upset a lady with my previous call to her home, and I also wondered what I would say, and what your father's reaction would be to me calling him. I knew that the area I was calling this time was near Chelmsford, but I had never been there, and I knew that it was quite a long way from where I was living in Milton Keynes.

Anyway with my mind made up, I had to bravely face yet another challenge. I lifted the telephone with a little bit of fear and trepidation at what might happen that day. I had already upset one family by asking them, and I knew that I was concerned about speaking to your dad, but I had to do this; I had to make this call. And as you can imagine, at the same time I was also excited that this call may mean that I would have direct contact with my three daughters once again.

So I rang the telephone number, was this the right one? And much to my surprise when the telephone was answered, it sounded like the voice of a very young person answering the telephone. I knew for certain then that it was not your father that I was speaking to, what a relief that was!

I did not know who it was that I was speaking to, but it turned out that I was speaking to your brother, because he was the person who had answered the telephone that day. I hadn't planned or thought of what I might say, and the first thing that came into my head was to ask if I could speak to Ann. Your brother replied that Ann did not live there anymore. Now at that my heart was really racing when I heard his reply, and I began trembling; and I had to think really quickly. I knew that I wasn't speaking to your father, and the thought came into my head, perhaps he may come in at any minute and stop the call, so my next question was, "Can I please speak to Grace?" and I then received the same reply. I was over the moon with excitement! I was now certain that I had found the right telephone number, but I still had to do some quick thinking, and the only thing that came in to my head at the time was, "Would you please give me a telephone number for Grace?" Your brother did not know who he was speaking to, and without any hesitation at all, he immediately looked up Grace's number and he gave it to me.

I will never be able to explain to you how I felt that day, I stood there in my living room, and my search was over. At that moment I had in my hand my daughter's telephone number, and I just couldn't take it in. This was now seventeen years after that awful day, the day your father arrived at the bungalow in Bolton and took you away from me: the day when he told me that he was taking you for a four week holiday. My friend who was there with me at the time was so very happy for me. This was such a long time in coming, and the day had finally arrived.

So armed with this new number, the next thing that I had to do was try to telephone and speak to Grace. So I did this next, and I was so pleased to be able to speak to Grace, she was three and a half years old when I last saw or spoke to her. She was quite surprised and also a bit shocked at my telephone call, but when I spoke to her, she said that she believed straight away that she was speaking to her mother; she said that no-one else was likely to call and say this.

I knew then that Grace was pleased, and it was then that she invited me down to Chelmsford to her home, so that I could meet with both her and her sisters!

You can imagine what I felt like when I went out that evening. I went to the party that was being held for my friend and I was so excited at the prospect of meeting my girls, that I couldn't get it out of my head. All of the other people who were there that night were also very pleased and excited for me; including the gentleman who was leaving. I think that we ended up having a double celebration that evening.

After having a really good time at the party, I went home that evening knowing that all I had to do was wait for a short time, as I knew then that I would be meeting all of my three daughters the following day at Grace's house.

I was so very excited the next day when I woke up, I can't even remember what day of the week it was now, many things are a wee bit of a blur to me by now, but I do remember waking up and immediately I remembered that this would be the first time that I would have seen or even spoken to any of you for seventeen long years.

I knew that your memory of me would have well faded by this time, as you were only little children when your father took you away that day. I did not have a clue as to how you would all be thinking. I expected that anything you had been told about me would have been negative, and I suppose I was thinking the very worst about that!

But here I was in my own home, and at last I had your address. I knew that this was the day that I was going to knock on a door somewhere in Chelmsford, and come face to face with each one of you again. This was a bit like the program, 'Long Lost Families' as far as I can think.

My friend turned up as he promised, as he had said that he would drive me over to Chelmsford to where Grace was living. This was to make it easier, and to save me driving that day. I was really excited and so looking forward to this moment when I would meet my family once again. He was also so pleased that he would be able to be like a fly on the wall that day! He wanted to see how our meeting went, and to know what happened, and also so very pleased that he could be a part of what was a big and momentous occasion for me that day.

So we journeyed on our way, one mile, then another, then another etc., I had not been to Chelmsford before, so everything was a bit like going into the unknown for me that day. We finally made it, we had now arrived in Chelmsford, and all we had to do was find the house that Grace and Joy lived in. I don't think that there was such a thing as satellite navigation in those days, but we managed to find the house fairly easily.

How exciting was this? I couldn't take it in, after spending so long visiting the Milton Keynes Library, at last I had this wonderful day to enjoy!

Anyway we finally reached the street, we found the door, many thoughts were rushing around in my head that day. Your father had probably heard about my telephone call to his home, and to Grace. Would he be here? But no matter what happened, I knew that I must knock on that door that I had just reached that day.

And here I was, I started to knock on the door, and then of course the door was suddenly opened, and standing there in front of me was a young lady who was a bit taller than me. Because she was taller than me, my first thoughts were that this must be my oldest daughter Ann, but it turned out that the young lady who opened the door was my youngest daughter Joy, and I hadn't seen her since she was about one-year old.

Joy took me to the upstairs part of the house and into the living room, and it was there that I met my other two daughters Ann and Grace. We all hugged and then the first place that we headed for was the kitchen. While we were still talking together, we made a cup of tea and then all four of us sat in the middle of the living room floor on the carpet. We all huddled together, and we must have spent some hours talking together. I think that everyone wanted to cover the last seventeen years at that first meeting.

How wonderful was that for all of us!

What did we talk about? Obviously my mind is rather a blank on this, everything just came rushing out of us, and I cannot remember the conversations, but it was no wonder, we all had such a lot of time to make up for!

And so that was the day that we met up again after seventeen long years. Grace and Joy lived in this house that I was now in. I remember on that day, that Joy showed me around her bedroom, and my daughter Ann told me that she had travelled over from the Cambridge area, as she and another girl owned a house there.

And of course my girls wanted to know everything that had happened, but how could everything that had happened be explained away in one evening? The many things that had caused it to happen, plus the seventeen years apart is a lot of ground to cover in one evening!

I was so very pleased to hear that my girls had spent some time trying to trace me, hearing that meant such a lot to me, even although they had not succeeded in this. What I was also so pleased about, was that they all accepted me that evening, they all knew that they had met up with their mother after all of those years apart.

Joy told me that she had thought that the babysitter was her real mum, until she was told at about age nine that she was not the babysitter's sister. Joy also told me that after she was told this, she always wanted to meet me!

And here we were, reunited after seventeen years, and this was just the beginning of the rest of our future!

After we had a catch up that day, we all had a walk to the nearest eating house, and we spent a nice evening there, until it was time for me to travel home once again.

So after this first meeting we continued to meet up, both in Ann's home and in my home in Milton Keynes, we attended a few of our church functions together, and I had the opportunity and pleasure of introducing my lovely daughters to many of my friends both there and later in my home.

I think that it was fairly obvious to all of us, that your father was not happy that we had met up again. He had obviously no intention of letting me know that you were all living in England, and if I had not found you, he would have been a much happier person!

Can you remember the party that I arranged for Joy's birthday at my home in Milton Keynes? Her father forbade her to come to the party, and Ann and Grace joined both my friends and me for the evening that we had planned for her. Later on in the evening there was a knock on the door, and there was your father standing on my doorstep with Joy, she had finally persuaded him to let her come, and on that evening he also joined us all for that evening of celebration. I found that such a strange evening, it was the first time I had been with all of the people who I thought of as my family, in so very many years.

I almost felt that I belonged, and that we all belonged together, this was where I ought to have been, it was such a really strange feeling!

And of course, you all know what happened after this!

Epilogue

I am sure that at least two of my children must have wondered at times "What if that had happened to me?", as two of my children each have two children of their own, and they must surely have gone through this thought process at some time.

I just want them to know that it would be the same for them, or any mother who lost her children, that they were always in my thoughts, there was always something missing from my life. I had lived for many years with an empty and lonely feeling deep within me!

I had accepted that I may never see you all again, but somewhere deep within my thoughts, I always believed that you would have a special protection that we asked to have for you just after you were born. I continued hoping that we would meet again, and tried my best to get on with my life, trying to keep myself going, hoping for the day when we would all meet up once again, and I think that I always believed that we would!

Probably the most important thing to me all of the time, was that I try to keep myself right, try to keep my beliefs and faith, and if it wasn't for this, and the support that I had from the other people I knew, I know that I would not have made it. It has not been an easy road through to here, but I am glad that I made it through, and am so happy that I met the lovely young ladies who are my daughters once again!

I have told you of my journeys and the places that I have lived, I have told you of how I felt, and you can perhaps imagine what the loss of my children did to me as a person. I was once told that I shouldn't have survived all that I went through, but here I am telling you the story, and I'm still very much alive!

From your point of view, I understand how hard it must be to think of me as your mum, but I did give birth to you, and although you do not know it, I never stopped loving you at any time. I know though that what happened must also have had a devastating effect on each of you.

I know that your dad and the babysitter married in Denmark, and that sometime after we all met again, she decided that she would leave him. I know that she has since then remarried and that she now lives abroad.

But what a trauma it must all have been, my little daughters had all of that upset in their young lives, it must have been really hard for them!

My daughter Grace lives in Australia, and she doesn't have any contact with me; that is her choice. I think that my oldest daughter who lives in Scotland, thinks of me more as a friend, and my youngest daughter who lives nearer to me, does call me mum, and I am always sure that when I see her, that she is very happy to see me and spend some time with me.

Two of my daughters have two children, so I am now a grandmother of four little children.

Sadly, I can't tell this story from the point of view of my children, I only know my own side and what happened to us, perhaps there's another story out there somewhere! But as a person, I have really regretted not having had the wonderful experience of raising my children, and of seeing them as they were growing up.

I can remember the first time that I visited Ann in her home in Cambridge, she had quite a number of pictures hanging on the hall wall of her home, and these showed the different stages that they had gone through as children, and it hit me just how much I had missed of their lives. I would have loved to see then growing up, and sharing all of the things that young people go through in their lives. My little children were now grown up young ladies. I had missed sharing their joys and their sorrows, and in fact in sharing their childhood and the many things that life brought to them. But I can say that I have had both the joy and excitement of meeting with them once again, and getting to know them, and I am so very proud of each one of them!

After my daughters were taken from me, one of my own sisters and her husband offered to take some Glasgow strong boys to snatch my children back. But you know if this had happened, I know their father, and the children would then have lived a life of backwards and forwards, and probably someone would have been killed in the process. But I thank her for that offer, I have not forgotten about that.

But what did it do for the other people who were involved in the stealing of my children, the ones who helped their father over the years, the ones who supported him in what he wanted? It must have made them very secretive about what they did. I expect that they had to lie at times to cover their tracks, and it also made them partly responsible for the kidnapping of my three children, and for the losses that we have all had as people. Because we will never be able to regain that mother-daughter relationship that we should have had.

These people listened to lies, helped and supported a very clever person who deliberately and cleverly lied and cheated his way out of everything. And they sadly allowed an elderly couple to have to say to a minister of the church, knowing that he was aware that they had the information, that they didn't want to get involved. It took me a long time after he asked them to find my children. They would have known that I was trying to find out where they were, there must have been some conversations between them and your father, and possibly other people during that period of time. And yet not one of them came to me, and told me where you were living.

I wonder sometimes if the people who helped and supported him over the years would have managed if this had been done to them, would they have turned the other cheek, and lived happily without the God given right that it is to look after and care for their offspring? That is what they supported and helped him to do to me!

But as I said before, it is not the purpose of this book to name names. I will not publicly identify anyone of these people who helped your father over the years, they know who they are, and they were unfortunately taken in by someone who was very clever and extremely devious.

And what about the Davis girl herself? She was young, and she was pretty, and she was like a bird in a gilded cage, she saw something that she wanted, and she took it. I know that he schooled her from an extremely early age, and he probably thought that he would get away with it, as some others did at that time. But you know, passions get aroused, and girls sometimes get themselves pregnant, and everyone else has to suffer the consequences. I fully believe though that she knew what she was doing at the time, she was very advanced for her age, but later when the pressure came, she couldn't take this and she fled the nest.

I have accepted now that after all these years of separation from my children, that we cannot have that true mother and daughter relationship that most of my friends seem to have with their children. This hurts me every time I think about it, but I still continue to have a song in my heart. I count my blessings that I know my children once again, I am so pleased that I met up with them again. I know that I will always be blamed for failing, and I do accept this! Sometimes I think that it would have been nice if someone who helped him had the courage to face me, and to apologise to me for the help that they gave him, and also continued to give him after he kidnapped my children!

Yes, wouldn't it be so nice to have had that one apology, for all the pain and the anguish that they put me through all of these years!

And what did ruining our family do for the father of my three children? He probably thought that he was in the right, that it was no big deal! Well, with his actions he really did become that little word that starts with a 'P'......you know the one, he had sex with a minor, albeit it was what she wanted too. He was a very clever liar, a cheat, a bully, a wife beater, a kidnapper, a thief who stole my lovely babies and everything else that I had spent the years that we had shared together working for. Yes, he took away all of my hopes and dreams! He had learned all of the tricks of how to get his own way, and there was no truth in him! What a disappointment he would have been to his parents and to his sister, who I know he loved very much. Do I hate him? No I do not; I would not waste my energy on hating him. I could even feel sorry for him, fancy having all of that on your conscience!

But now the time has come, I want you my daughters to know how and why it all happened, why you were brought up in Copenhagen when both of your parents were brought up in Scotland, and I want you to know that I did love you then, and I still do now!

I am sorry for all of the mistakes that I have made, and also very deeply sorry that I was so very afraid of your father at that time of my life. I know that it is wrong to be that afraid of anyone, but at the time when these things were happening to me, I was very afraid, as he had previously threatened all of our lives. No-one messes with your dad, he doesn't look tough, but he is so very clever, and I took his threats seriously.

I know that many people will probably consider that I am a soft touch, why was I so afraid of your father, why did I allow this to happen? I know that I may have 'prize fool' written over my forehead. I took a monstrous hit as a person, but yes, I have tried over the years to do what I believed was right. I truly believed that our lives were in danger that day, and I still wonder at times where the axe went that the Landlord said was taken from his garage!

There was no pool of blood that day, with brute force he got what he wanted just as he usually did. But you know what, I got something too. I know that I did not share my childrens' childhood, or their love, <u>but my children are all still alive,</u> and they now have families of their own, and I as a mother I am so very pleased for them!

You know I believe that my little old mother was very wise, she once said in a conversation with me, that such cleverness is next to cunning, and that cunning is next to evil.

She didn't get it far wrong, did she!

Anyway prize fool or not, who will be found wanting when the saints go marching in?

Thankfully we are all given the chance to walk the walk, and to be sorry for the mistakes that we have made!

So I have come to the end of this story, and full circle to when I was just sixteen years old, and at that time as you now know, I joined my first concert party, and I did this because as you know, I loved to sing. The man who ran the concert party was called Alex, and he stood up on the stage on many occasions and sang this song, I think that it is meant to be a love song, so I have changed the words a bit, but it is quite appropriate for me and my life.

'I'm not good looking, I'm not too smart, I may be fooling but I've got a heart…

Don't laugh at me cause I'm a fool, I know it's true, yes I'm a fool, no-one seems to care, I'd give the world to share my life with others who really love me.... I see them all sharing their love, but my lucky star still hides above, some day may-be my star will shine on me, don't laugh at me cause I'm a fool!'

I can remember when I was a young woman just starting out in life, I wasn't so smart, or even good looking, but with excitement and happiness and with hope in my heart, and with my whole future stretching out before me, I jumped on to a bantam motor bike, and throwing my arms around a young man of eighteen, and hugging Rusty our jacket, I was thrilled and excited, and even hopeful that our journey through life would be a good one.

But the end of a perfect day became an unhappy life sentence!

As there was no such luck with that one for me.